DESIGNING YOUR
DREAM

Discovering the destiny that's been fashioned for you !

Gina La Morte

Oinabiz Media
New York, New York

Oinabiz Media
New York, New York

ISBN 978-0-9833591-4-2
eBook ISBN 978-0-9833591-3-5

Printed in the United States of America

Cover design by Jeremiah Lanska, 2 Intense Design
www.2IntenseDesign.com
Cover photograph by Anthony Bagileo

10 9 8 7 6 5 4 3 2 1

First Edition March 2015

Dedicated to my children;
Sebastian Bo, Hope Rain, and Isabella Star.
You are my biggest dream, my loves and my life.

To all of my dreamers;

Every great dream begins with a dreamer. Always remember, you have within you the strength, the patience, and the passion to reach for the stars and change the world.

-Harriet Tubman

A quote that set me free...
don't be afraid of your light.

Our deepest fear is not that we are inadequate. Our
deepest fear is that we are powerful beyond measure.
It is our light, not our darkness that most frightens us.
We ask ourselves, who am I to be brilliant, gorgeous,
talented, fabulous? Actually, who are you not to be?
You are a child of God. Your playing small does not serve
the world. There's nothing enlightened about shrinking so
that other people won't feel insecure around you.
We are all meant to shine, as children do. We were born
to make manifest the glory of God that is within us.
It's not just in some of us; it's in everyone. And as we let
our own light shine, we unconsciously give other people
permission to do the same. As we're liberated from our
own fear, our presence automatically liberates others.

—*Marianne Williamson*
A Return to Love

CONTENTS

INTRODUCTION

Everyone has oceans to fly if they have the heart. Is it reckless? Yes, but what do dreams know of boundaries?
~ Amelia Earhart

Everyone has a dream. Dreams are visions for your life placed in your heart by God to help you discover your destiny. I believe we all have a destiny and purpose we were born for, but it is ours to discover. The dreams you have inside of your heart are placed there for a reason. Do not dismiss them, as they are stepping-stones to walk you into your divine purpose. Think of them as your compass. They will guide you to that very thing you are born to do. However, many people have kept their dreams locked away for various reasons. Some have buried them because of the pain of their past; others believe they will never come true so they don't even try; some have a fear of failure; others have a fear of success; some get sidetracked with the issues of life, staying stuck in a safe job in order to survive and provide; while others have a dream much greater than themselves and simply do not know how to begin in order to see that dream fulfilled. Some people are blessed with multiple dreams, but they live with the frustration of not knowing which one to start off with first, leaving them unable to ever start at all. I can speak to the dreams in your heart because I have walked this path myself. I have been blessed to live out many of my own dreams and I can tell you there is no way anyone can help you birth a dream unless they have birthed one themselves. I don't mean walking it out like just seeing it happen or telling you how to do it, I mean literally experiencing it all—the good and the bad, the pretty and the ugly. The journey to a dream come true doesn't always smell of roses along the entire way, sometimes there are thorns, and sometimes you get pricked. The most amazing thing I can say today is that I know how it feels to get stuck by some of those thorns, but I also know how gratifying it feels to bloom into a rose even after the pricking. I have experienced every step there is to know about how to see a dream go from an idea into fulfillment. I have witnessed that divinely planted dream seed blossom into a full fruit-bearing tree. I am living proof that if you don't give up, if you don't cave in, if you don't quit, but just keep moving forward, one step at a time, no matter what obstacles come in your path, you will see your dreams become a reality.

That leads me to share with you what I believe are the two very important purposes for writing this book. One is to pull out the very 'destiny' inside of you and get you walking in what I believe you are born to do. Two, is to share with you the process of what the journey to a dream is *REALLY* like, and encourage you not to quit along the way! You see, the majority of your life will be spent waiting for your dream to happen. During that time of waiting it may take years, even decades, to see your dream come to pass. Throughout that journey, there will be countless opportunities to become completely frustrated, feel extremely discouraged, and simply want to give up because things aren't happening quite like you've imagined. That being said, the secret to success lies in just two simple requirements: for you to believe, and for you to persevere. I believe this book will guide you through the steps of instruction that will help you break past the barriers you are facing, and unlock the dreams in your heart. Let's take this journey together to see your dreams fulfilled and live the life you've imagined!

Dreaming with you,

Gina

Part One

Designing Your Dream: Discovering The Destiny That's Been Fashioned For You

Chapter 1
How Fashion Designed
My Dream

Every great dream begins with a dreamer.
Always remember, you have within you the strength, the
patience, and the passion to reach for the stars
and change the world.
~Harriet Tubman

I spent my childhood dreaming. It's what I did. It seemed like a full-time occupation and I loved every minute of it. People always called me a dreamer and could recall stories that I would share with them as a little girl about my dreams of one day owning my own fashion magazine and working in the fashion industry so I could help "make people look pretty." People also told me that I needed to be realistic so that I wouldn't become disappointed in life. They were wrong. No one, but no one, was going to ever tell me that I couldn't accomplish my dreams.

I recall an epitaph that I had pasted up in my high school locker that read, *"You'll either grow up to become someone who changes the world, a fashion designer, a star; or you'll spend the rest of your life in front of the television."* It was a funny thing because deep inside I knew this to be true. I had two sides of me, each vastly different from the other. One side was the big city fashionista dreamer; the other was a tree-loving New Jersey beach girl with an old soul who just wanted to spend hours watching the waves roll in. Growing up, I spent the majority of my life staring blissfully at those waves. They were my haven, my peace. But while staring into them I envisioned the very moment I would arrive at 17 years of age in New York City and become some fancy fashion girl who would one day influence women all over the world through fashion, and help them live their own dreams. Fast forward to today, all of those dreams came true, along with a host of others! Was I special? No! Was I focused? Yes! Were any of these dreams accomplished without an incredible amount of sacrifice and discipline? No! Did all of these dreams seem impossible at the time? Yes! Did all of my dreams require an act of faith? Double Yes! You see, when you dream dreams that are so much larger than yourself, you have to believe in the impossible, because there's no way in reality you can make them happen on your own. Yes, your dreams will require you to do the work(and way more work and sacrifice than you can ever imagine) but…for one, the work will never feel like work because you are doing what you love, and two, the impossible becomes possible when you put your faith in your Creator, believing that your dreams are a part of your destiny that's been designed just for you! By taking the steps to live out your dreams you are simply walking out what you were created for!

Best Dressed.

As a young girl, flipping through fashion magazines was one of my favorite pastimes. I dreamt of the day that I would be able to style a photo shoot and become editor-in-chief of some glamorous magazine. In my childhood bedroom, pages upon pages of magazines covered my walls, my closet doors, and every schoolbook and surface I could get my hands on. I was utterly obsessed with how the fashion stories were styled and how the models wore the clothes. I would countdown the days until the newest issue of *Vogue* would hit my mailbox so I could tear into it and create stories on my walls. I would put to-gether trend boards of color, style and looks & then would cut out inspirational words and powerful female messages, plastering them up over everything! I was enthralled with my own world of bliss and loved every minute of it. I was so obsessed with magazines and actually believed they were so precious that after I cut them all up I would then go out and buy another copy of the same magazine, seal it up in plastic wrap and pack it away so it would forever be untouched. I still have some of these issues saved today (pretty much every Kate Moss cover, all of the supermodel covers from *Vogue* and *Elle*, and all of the *Bazaar* covers when Liz Tilberis was at the helm!). Fashion, accessories, shoes, all of it was my life at that time. When you are young and have a dream you will do anything to get closer to it and become a part of what you're dreaming about! Aside from rummaging through magazines and creating trend-forecasting boards, my other fashion outlet was styling my own personal wardrobe. For fun, I created a fashion calendar where I would write down daily each one of my outfits, so that I was sure never to repeat the same one twice within the month (it sounds so crazy to me now!). It wasn't that I had too many clothes; rather it was *all* about my infatuation with styling. I loved the challenge of seeing how many outfits I could create by repurposing the same pieces when mixing them up with new ones, and then layering in different accessories to create new looks. At a young age, my mother taught me how to play around with fashion and make something look new even if it wasn't. I became a mix-master of accessorizing and editing. To me, fashion was never about the excess of always having to have more clothes, but rather it was always about creating great style in your own personal way. That's how I learned to become a true fashion stylist, and also what I believe won me the title of *'Best Dressed'* my senior year of High School. Even my classmates supported my passion for fashion and my deep desire to live out my dream of one day working as a stylist in New York City.

7

California Dreamin'.
In my junior year of High School I was part of a marketing program called *DECA*. The year I entered they held a national competition with the prize being an all-expense paid trip to California! At the time one of my biggest dreams, aside from attending the Fashion Institute of Technology in New York City, was to visit California. I definitely was California Dreamin' in my mind probably because of my love for the ocean and my fascination with the idealistic California lifestyle.

When I heard this was the prize, I was determined to do whatever it took to win my ticket to Cali! I entered the National Competition for Business Marketing and my project was to open up a surf shop in France's Cote D'Azur. My passion kicked into high gear to take this project over the top, so I had my father get in touch with the French consulate to help gather information about opening a retail business there. Everything about the project was done in real time, so I had to conduct myself as if I would actually be opening up this dream surf shop, including doing all of the marketing, demographics, business plan, and more. The excitement filled me as I pressed into my creative business side I never realized I had. However, all of my dreams almost came to a screeching halt when I learned that I would have to face my biggest fear in order to win this prize: public speaking! One of the requirements of winning was to present my business idea to a live group of discerning judges. This would be my first-ever public speaking experience and I was pretty much scared to death. At this time in my life I was an extremely shy person, so speaking in front of anyone was not something I felt very comfortable doing. In fact, I was so afraid to face my fear that I seriously considered giving up on this dream. Somewhere within me I had to make a conscious decision to choose my dream over my fear. I had to get my mind in a place (after much practice presenting in class and at home) where I felt my fear was worth facing for my dream. Finally, the day of the competition arrived. After two days of presentations in front of multiple strangers, I survived the public speaking and finally faced my fear! At that moment I realized that even if I didn't win my dream prize of going to

California, I had won for myself in conquering one of my biggest fears and finally becoming free of it.

When the time came to await the award ceremony, I became so nervous once again. Suddenly, I heard the judges announce the winners and I almost passed out as I heard my name being called! I had won 2nd place in the state of New Jersey competition and was awarded an all-expense paid trip to California to compete in the Nationals! In addition, because of my win I was also granted a full scholarship to Los Angeles's *FIDM*, which I ultimately turned down to attend my dream school, of New York City's *Fashion Institute of Technology* (but that's another story!).

Chapter 2
What's Your Original Design?

*Be who you were created to be, and
you will set the world on fire.*
~ *St. Catherine of Sienna*

There are over 70 billion fingerprints and not one of them is the same. We each have our own talents, abilities and gifts that make us unique and unlike anyone else. You are an original design, hand-crafted like a custom couture gown by the famous Designer of all creation. There is something that you are called to do better than anyone else in the world. That is why you don't ever have to worry about somebody copying you, because nobody can. No one in the world can ever be like you, no matter how hard they try, it's humanly impossible. The same goes for your dreams. Yes, there may be other people with similar ideas or concepts as yours, but only you have your unique custom take on it. It's your special flavor, point of view, and experiences that will make it your own.

Just look at fashion designers. It's fairly obvious that there are more than enough clothes in the world already created. However without fail, each year a new crop designer buds up, and suddenly the world finds a new reason to buy a new dress! Why? Because the designer comes to the table with their own unique perspective on fashion, and it's translated differently than anyone else has done before. So you see, the category of clothing remains the same, but the newness comes in the translation of a collection. This is why it doesn't matter what your dream is or how similar you think it may be to somebody else's. Your ideas and talent are all original to you, and so are your dreams.

What you love is part of what creates your original design. Everything that you like, that you enjoy, that you are naturally attracted to, everything that has special meaning to you; all of it has divine purpose and points to the direction of your dreams. Even the littlest things you take delight in, for example, the special cup that you like to drink your coffee in, the colors that make you feel happy, the scents that you love to smell, the scenery that you want to be surrounded by, your fashion style, the music you listen to, etc. Think about all of the things that make your heart smile. All of your loves actually point to the direction of your dreams, because it's the little things that paint the whole picture. I want you to spend some time journaling and exploring what makes your heart happy. By being intentional about your loves, you will be able to connect the dots and form a design around your dreams. It's taking your very essence and creating a collaborative picture around it to start the process of dreaming.

Your dreams derive out of your natural talents.
While nothing is impossible to those who believe, dreams are actually based in reality and are derived from the natural talents you were born with. Your natural skillset, whether you were born with it or have learned it over years of experience, will play the largest role in what you will be doing with your dream. For example, if you have a beautiful voice, pursuing a singing career is a real possibility. If you have a gift of organization, becoming head of operations or starting a planning company are options. Perhaps you're excellent at taking care of children, or have a natural talent for cooking and entertaining? Maybe you are constantly encouraging other people? Are there certain skills that come so naturally to you that you may not even see them as special? Many times our natural talents are such a 'natural' part of what we do daily that they don't seem like talents at all. I remember consulting with a client who shared, "Gina, I don't have anything

special about me. My life is like everyone else's. I am just a mom who runs the house, keeps everyone on schedule, makes sure this place stays organized, and I'm the go-to person who everyone calls when there's a problem." Wait, what? *Just* a mom? A life like everyone else's? Doing nothing special? Hmmmm...Just because you aren't out running a nation doesn't mean you're not running your own nation at home. What I hear from that is that you are a natural organizer, planner, teacher, encourager and problem solver! That's 5 major talents that may have come super easy to my client, however I know countless people who struggle with even being good at just one of these talents. Do you see how being successful in daily life is actually a gift and talent? Running an organized household, keeping people on schedule, having a listening ear, and being a mother are all qualities, special skills, that can be easily overlooked, however when taking a closer look you can easily see it takes talent. Sometimes our natural talents come so easily to us that we may not even realize they are unique gifts. If you struggle to see your own strengths, I want you to ask a close friend or family member who interacts with you on a regular basis about what they think you are good at. Sometimes loved ones can see the good qualities in us better than we can see them in ourselves. There's nothing wrong with getting a little help from your friends!

Don't get caught up in comparison.
I can remember as a young girl, like most females, I would compare myself to other girls who were different than me and wonder why I wasn't more like them. At that time, I was discovering who I was and was too immature to cherish my unique, authentic self that I eventually came to embrace. You see I had a very fiery personality. I was extremely passionate, driven and career-focused. There were many times when I felt like working towards my career was much more important than having fun. At times, I would get frustrated with myself for not being able to just 'live in the moment'. While I was wishing away these traits during my high school years, I soon realized, once I had arrived at college, that it was those very traits I

naturally possessed that were required for me to survive the competitive career spirit of New York City's fashion industry. I could have never have made it there had I not been so bold and driven. I realized that sometimes the very things that you want to change about yourself are the very things needed to accomplish your purpose. The qualities you wish weren't there when you were younger are the same qualities you will need as an adult, but you just aren't aware of it yet. Don't despise the parts of you that you may not yet understand, or may not be similar to someone else. Remember, everyone has his or her own original design, and just because everybody else may be going in one direction and you may be going in another, does not mean you are going in the wrong direction. You are on your own path, and one day it will make sense.

Don't let anyone steal your voice.
One day, I was watching Disney's *The Little Mermaid* with my daughter. There was a specific part in the film where the evil witch tries to get Ariel to give away her voice, attempting to convince her that she had plenty of other good qualities that could replace it. As she sang this dark song, speaking negative words over her, calling her "a poor, unfortunate soul," you begin to see Ariel is struggling to recognize her true identity. Ariel did not see who she really was, and had no idea of the value of keeping and protecting her voice. She was willing to trade her voice because during this time in her youth, when her destiny hadn't been revealed, she could not see that it was her voice that would connect her to her dream of finding her true love. Her voice symbolized the very essence of who she was created to be! If she lost her voice, she would forfeit her destiny! That's true for you too. At the core of your God-given dreams is your voice. We each have our own unique sound and recognizing its value and not allowing it to be stolen, by anyone for any reason, is what will keep you on the right path to your dream. There will be a time in your life when you will become tempted to give away your voice. You may be offered an opportunity to make your dream happen prematurely. Because you

want your dream to happen so badly, you are willing to take the first thing that comes your way, even if it's not 100% right. If this happens to you I want to remind you of this truth: *your dream will never require you to compromise the very essence of who you are in order to attain it*. It is essential that you never become so anxious to make your dream happen that you are willing to take the bait of a counterfeit dream. Rest assured, when it's your time for your dream to come true it will happen the right way. Nothing and no one can stop it or steal it. So hold on to your voice, because it's yours, and no one else has a right to it!

Chapter 3
Passion Leads To Your Purpose

*Life motivation comes from the deep longings in the heart,
and the passion to see them fulfilled urges you onward.*

~ Brian Simmons, Proverbs; The Passion Translation

I once heard someone say, "It's your passion that moves you. It's what burns you up inside, it's that fire in your belly. It is destiny inside of you that makes you want to do something to fix or improve that unjust situation." It is this spiritual emotion, described as the "fire in your belly", that leads you to your purpose. For example, have you ever felt so pumped up about something that you felt like you needed to tell everyone around you to 'do something' about it, yet no one else seems to care much about what you are sharing except for you? Well, that's because *you* are the one who is supposed to do something, not everyone else...*YOU*! That's why *you* have the passion for it, and the desire to take action in order to change it. Sometimes this very simple principle becomes too complicated to see because we fail to notice what's right in front of us. It's what you are passionate about that comes so naturally to you, and that's exactly what helps lead you to your purpose! So I ask you, what is that fire in your belly for? What are you yearning to do, fix or change? What is your passion that's leading you to your purpose?

Sometimes the fire burns for many things.
When I was younger I struggled for many years trying to figure out my purpose. I had been passionate about so many things in life that I felt like a mixed up puzzle, none of the pieces seemed to fit together. I had a passion for fashion, a heart for social justice, a desire to help others, and an appreciation of nature; yet somehow none of these things seemed to connect. It wasn't until after working for many years in the fashion industry that I could make sense of it all.

I will never forget the day that I was divinely downloaded the vision for my magazine. It was on that day that I saw every single one of my unrelated passions begin to weave themselves together into the most beautiful tapestry of a dream! Suddenly it all made sense! In that moment I realized that all of those years of varied experiences I had were not in vain. Had I not experienced them I would have never acquired all of the skills to be able to run my own magazine. I cannot even begin to explain the elation I felt seeing the puzzle pieces of my career come together. I know there are plenty of other people who are like me, facing the same challenge of not understanding how all of their unique talents can actually work together for a divinely designed purpose. To help you figure it out, I came up with a series of questions that I want you to ask yourself to help you find your passion and locate that fire in your belly! Take some time to really meditate on these questions. I know they will help you.

What do you have a fire in your belly for?

What or who do you feel a burden for?

What are you yearning to do but feels too big to accomplish on your own?

What would you do in your wildest dreams?

What do you daydream about while you are at work?

When you stare at the sky, what are you imagining?

What unfinished dreams do you have floating around in your head?

What would you do if you had all the money in the world?

What would you be doing if you had every connection you needed to accomplish it?

What is your deepest heart's desire that nobody knows about?

What would you shout from a mountaintop and tell the world?

If you could do anything right now and create your dream life, what would that look like?

Purpose; it's what you are designed for.
Right before his death, one of Dr. Myles Munroe's quotes went viral. *"The greatest tragedy is not death; the greatest tragedy is life without a purpose."* It's so true. How can we live life without having a reason to live it? I think we all are born with the God-given desire to want to know the answer to the question, 'Why am I here?'" We long for that feeling of fulfillment that comes along with finding out this answer, and the satisfaction of actually living it out. Without a sense of purpose, we can lose our hope. It's that feeling of purpose that drives our passion, and gives us hope for the future. The best way to find your purpose is to follow the passion that's in your heart and let it lead you to the very thing you were designed for. A life with purpose is a life worth living.

Your passion for your dream is contagious.
Did you know that sharing the excitement of your own dream actually stirs up the dreams in someone else? Your passion becomes

contagious because it ignites a fire in others, inspiring others to believe in their own dreams. Sometimes your passion will even fan the flame of someone else's heart to come along with you for the ride of your own dream. Dreams become contagious to another person when they watch you reach for the stars and see you soaring, moving closer to that dream coming true! Dreams become infectious when you share the passion for your dream from your heart, not from your head. People actually can feel and see the difference! You never know whose fire you will light up and whose flame you'll fan by sharing your passion for your dream.

Passion helps complete the project.
Did you know that it's your passion for what you do that will help you see your project through to completion? Passion is that force of nature that keeps the fire burning within and drives you to finish what you have started. I love the proverb "A passive person won't even complete a project. But a passionate person makes good use of his time wealth and energy." The truth is that anyone can have a dream, but not everyone will have the passion to complete it. I believe that you are that passionate person who wants to see their dream come true and see it through to the end.

Chapter 4
Your Dream Isn't Only About You

If you can't feed 100 people then just feed one.
~Mother Teresa

Your dreams were not put in you to simply fulfill a selfish desire; they were designed to be a gift to others. Dreams, while they initially seem selfish by nature, always somehow benefit and help someone else. All dreams, big or small, world changing or seemingly insignificant, will inevitably impact another person's life. The wonderful part of living a dream is that, while it may be the solution to someone else's problem, you will reap the rewards of feeling the satisfaction of accomplishing it. Just like Mother Teresa, who had a dream to feed starving children and care for orphans, or Martin Luther King Jr. who had a dream for others to be treated fairly and walk free without prejudice, dreams can provide freedom, healing and deliverance to an entire generation while only attempting to help just one. One person's dream can change both nations and individuals. Going after your dreams can be driven by the desire not only to make your world a better place, but also someone else's. If your dream only helps one other person, it is a success.

Dreams solve a problem for someone else.
You've heard the phrase "Make somebody's dream come true."

I believe this is a popular phrase because if we approach living out our dreams with a pay-it-forward attitude then it becomes quite encouraging to go after them with real fervor. Dreams that become successful will always help someone else solve a problem and aren't just selfish in motive. Perhaps you desire to become an expert closet organizer; you are solving someone else's problem of lack of time and organization skills. Or maybe by creating your dream company you could become one of the best employers to work for, creating new jobs for those in need of work. Perhaps your dream will help students learn in a new way or give children the opportunity to attend school if they haven't before? Every dream solves a problem or fulfills a dream for someone else. So ask yourself the question, "In whose life will my dream make a difference?" Let your answer be a stepping-stone to lead you into your dreams.

Dreams create legacy.
Some dreamers are pioneers. They are trying to do something new, lead change in a positive direction and desire to leave a legacy behind. I know that I am passionate about wanting to leave a legacy for my own children. I'm also passionate about leaving a legacy to a generation of people impacted by the good that I do here on Earth. When thinking about your dreams realize they have the potential to be world changing and at the same time can impact one special person, forever. Why would you want to do something that only benefits you when you could also help someone else? Even if it is just one person whose life you could improve for the better, isn't that worth it? I take that legacy quite seriously. I let that thought process lead me to my next dream because I recognize that what I have been given on this earth can and should be used to help somebody else. Think about your dream today and the legacy you'd want to leave behind. Whether it is for your children or the next generation, you have the power to be a pioneer and have your dreams create change for the better.

Chapter 5
Career vs. Calling

Jobs come and go, but a calling is something you were given the moment you were born. You can lose a job, but you can't lose your calling.
~ *Marianne Williamson*

Your calling is where your talents and burdens collide. Your career is what you do for money. Your calling is what you were born for. Sometimes people believe their career is their calling, and it can be, however, many times the current role you are playing is ultimately training you *for* your calling. Your calling is something worth pursuing because it's your purpose in life. Your dreams are usually directed towards your calling. You have these desires in your heart that drive you towards doing a certain job, and it feels like what you are born, or called, to do. It's so precious to be walking in what you were born for, rather than being stuck in a career that doesn't fulfill you. You will feel a connection to your calling. It 'calls' out to you to seek and find it. Search for it. Dig deep to discover it. It will be one of the most rewarding experiences you will have in life.

Imagining the impossible.
As children we do imaginary play. We may proclaim things like, "When I grow up I'm going to be…" We are free to believe the impossible and create ourselves into people without limits. We

imagine things that have never existed before and believe they can become real. There is no one telling us, "No, that can't be done!" Being an imaginary child is a limitless experience without boundaries. It allows our creativity to flourish. It's when we are children that we discover our dreams because of this free flowing creativity. As we become adults, the road of life taints us along the way, and for the most part our dreams become fleeting. We gather up experiences that then cause us to bury our dreams and lock them away. In the bible, we are asked to have child-like faith and believe like little children. Could this reminder exist because once we become an adult we are tainted with the facts of life, thus becoming inhibited from dreaming the big dreams God has planted in our heart since birth? I believe that the majority of this pressure comes against our child-like faith when we begin applying to college. Suddenly we are required to answer the age-old question of "What do I want to do when I grow up?" It's as if all of a sudden we are expected to magically know what we are going to do with the rest of our lives in that moment. However, life isn't like that. We discover our identities and purpose along our journey, many times discovering *after* college what we really want to do in life. And even then it may evolve! The famous 'college question' creates so much pressure to hurry up and decide who we are that many times we end up pursuing a degree we really don't want, which leads us into a career that we never imagined ourselves in.

Don't be afraid to answer these questions candidly. It's ok to not be in the place where you want to be yet and still be designing your dream. This entire dreaming experience is a process. The key is to get you to the place where you can break past all of the barriers and move forward into making it happen. To help you discover the difference between your career and your calling, I want you to ask yourself these questions:

Do you feel passionate about what you are currently doing?

Do you feel like you are making a contribution in the current place you are working?

Do you feel frustrated and have a knowing that there is 'more'?

Do you currently feel complete fulfillment where you are at in your life?

Are you being a positive influence or are you under the influence of negativity?

Do you feel like you are making a difference in someone's life or in the world?

Balance is the key to transition.

Maxwell Maltz said *"Man maintains his balance, poise, and sense of security only as he is moving forward."* Making the decision to start pursuing your dreams and move forward towards the next step of exiting your career requires a delicate balancing act. The transition will bring some major lifestyle changes, and it's imperative that you understand what these changes are before you decide to take the leap. I've learned that you can never be too extreme in your actions, quitting everything all at once. You must discern when the proper timing is to resign from your current career to pursue your calling. To figure out when the right timing will be, some important questions to ask yourself are: Is your current job your only source of income? Does your current job support your family? Is your current job training you with the skills you will need for your calling? If you've answered 'yes' to any of these questions then you do not want to hurry up and quit your career. You must know when it's the right time to move forward for two very important reasons: one is that you don't want to end up struggling financially, and two; you don't want to cut short any opportunities that may be training you for your dream. The reality is that there may be a transition period where you are holding down a full-time job and working on your dream at the same time. Or, you may have to work part-time to keep yourself financially secure, while the other part of your time is spent working on your dream. No matter what the case, you need to weigh out all of your options and see how you can make it work on paper before you ever make that decision in reality. It's truly essential for you to create a realistic financial plan for how you are going to pay your bills without a full-time job or with only a part-time job, while you are pursuing your dream. However on the flip side of that, I believe and I have seen some people step out in faith to move towards their dream without a job, without financial security, and without knowing the big picture. Trust me, if this happens to you (and it happened to me!) you will *know* in your spirit that this is what you are supposed to be doing because you will feel a supernatural peace upon making your decision. If this is your path, you may initially feel fearful and extremely out of your comfort zone, but that feeling of trepidation won't last very long. If you are truly ready to follow your calling, all of those negative emotions will soon be replaced with a peaceful excitement and enthusiasm. Either way, as long as you maintain balance during your transition, you will be successful when it's time to move out of your career and into your calling.

Letting go of the past to walk forward into your future.
I remember what a juggling act the transition was for me while I was working towards my dream of launching *Boho*. For the past 8 years I had been working for myself with the very first fashion company I created back in 2000, a website called *TheStyleDoctor. com*. Throughout that time I had developed some pretty powerful partnerships along with a healthy roster of client relationships that turned into friendships. I was beyond blessed to have built my dream career working as a Celebrity Fashion Stylist for magazines, television networks and luxury retailers like *O, the Oprah magazine, People StyleWatch, MTV, CBS, ABC, Neiman Marcus, Nordstrom* and more. At the time I was married and had my first child. I loved being a new mom and wanted to spend as much time with my son as possible, so we chose not to have a nanny. While we did have family to help babysit

at times, everyday life was a constant juggling act between the two of us working parents. During the day, with my son on my hip or while he was napping, I would work for my *Style Doctor* clients. Then, in the evenings after I put my son to bed, it was back to work trying to launch the dream of *Boho*, sometimes until 2:30am! Before I knew it, I would be back up at 6:30am the next day to start it all over again. Eventually something had to give. At that point I had to make the tough decision to walk away from some of my favorite clients and a dream I worked on for almost a decade! It was so hard letting any of them go, not only for financial reasons, but because I had built such wonderful relationships, and frankly I loved my job! I did not want to say goodbye to anyone, but I realized if I didn't let go of my past I would not be able to walk forward into my future.

I knew in my heart it was time to launch my new dream, but in my head it made absolutely NO sense for me to walk away from this steady stream of well-paying clients who became friends. I had to choose to move past my fear of the unknown and simply follow what I believed was right. I'll never forget the day I had scheduled a lunch in NYC to tell my last and most favorite client I was moving on and could no longer work for them. Her words were like sweet honey to my soul. She said, "Gina, you have to go for your dream. If you don't do it now, you will never know what you may miss out on!" She was right! After that day I felt free to move forward, and everything fell into place with the launching of my new magazine. I literally felt like I had finally stepped into my *DESTINY*! It was completely surreal. In that moment I realized when launching a dream that you can't have one foot in your past and one in your future. You must have both feet facing forward, and be willing to give up what's good in order to receive what's best.

Chapter 6
Get Activated

Over the years I have developed a series of exercises that help activate the dreams within us. I believe they will help you recall that child-like faith we all need to have in order to pursue our dreams. You can't design your dream if you can't identify it first, so I want you to look at these exercises as a fun and creative part of the dreaming process. I'd like you to allow yourself the freedom and open heart to participate fully in this activity without distraction or any personal judgments. No matter what stage you are at along your dream journey, devoting the time and energy to answering these questions to the best of your ability will greatly improve the experience you have during this exploratory phase. To get prepared, I suggest you designate a special journal, an area on your iPad or tablet, or download one of my favorite apps called *Evernote* (I use it to organize and brainstorm almost everything!) to answer these questions. No matter how you like to work, find something to 'claim your space' and make it your official devotion area to start writing your dream vision down.

1. Think back to when you were a free spirited child.

Think about everything that you dreamt about before the reality of life stepped in and may have clouded it.

    a.   What did you imagine yourself doing one day?
    b.   How did you see your life?
    c.   What did you think about the most?
    d.   What made you feel most free?
    e.   Who did you pretend to be?
    f.   Was there anyone you desired to emulate?
    g.   Did you have dreams of becoming someone special ?
    h.   Do you remember what your personality was like as a child?
    i.   Was there anything you imagined doing that you dismissed because someone had told you that it was impossible or impractical?

I want you to journal everything that comes to mind, even if you think it's meaningless or trivial. Some of you may struggle with this question because your dreams may be buried so deep that you may not even remember that they exist. This actually happened to me. One of my childhood dreams was to have my own fashion magazine. However, for some reason I had buried this dream so deep in my heart that I hadn't even remembered it was there! Fast-forward 20 years later, one random day, while I was on assignment working on location in a retail store for another magazine interviewing fashion expert Carson Kressley, I had a flashback. While quietly standing around the store prepping for my interview, a random, yet long-time veteran salesperson at Nordstrom walked up to me, stared me straight in the eyes and asked me in a stern, but affirming, voice "Did you ever think of having your own magazine?" I became frozen in my tracks. What did he say? It was as if years of my life had come flooding back to me in that moment. How did he know this? Who was this man? And, most importantly, how did I ever forget that I had this lifelong dream in my heart? Boom! It was like destiny and reality collided. I felt as if God sent me a sign to remind me of one of my biggest childhood dreams that I had forgotten. After I completed that interview I went home and gave my two weeks' notice. It was like fire hit my belly and I knew with everything in me that I had to take the leap and go for my dream.

Nine months later, I launched my own magazine, *Boho*. It was a pioneer publication; a first of it's kind. It was an environmentally friendly fashion focused magazine, made from 100% post-consumer waste paper (using only tree-free paper from recycled garbage). We inspired dreamers everywhere to live a more sustainable lifestyle of giving back and going green. Our vision was shown through fashion, beauty and food. We launched in the biggest bookstores and on newsstands nationwide, right alongside *Oprah* and *Vogue*. We landed a contract with one of the world's top international magazine distributors and were distributed in 37 countries in addition to the USA. *Boho* was sold in *Whole Foods, Barnes & Noble, Target, CVS, Duane Reade* and thousands of chains across the world.

THAT DAY, MY BIGGEST DREAM WAS IGNITED BY A TOTAL STRANGER. That experience made me realize three very important things that I had never thought about before. One was that I almost let one of my biggest dreams die because I had let years of fear and unbelief tell me that if a dream seemed impossible it could never come true (how wrong I was!). Two, I realized that even a total stranger can be used as a catalyst to speak life back into your buried dreams (I consider these types of people angels, even though they are real). Three, and most importantly, I experienced first-hand how God, who puts these dreams in your heart, will never *EVER* let a dream die and allow you to miss your destiny, even if He has to use a total stranger to remind you of what you forget! Today, I am beyond grateful that I was open-minded enough to listen to a stranger's encouraging words and be given the grace to have one of my biggest dreams come true.

2. What would you do if you had no limits?
Living a dream can be an exciting and adventurous experience, but for some people dreaming can conjure up negative thoughts, thoughts like, "*I can't afford it. I'm afraid. It's impossible. I don't have the*

time", etc. What I want you to do is remove all of the limits from your mind and allow yourself the freedom to dream as if all of your dreams were a guaranteed success. Start by asking yourself these five simple questions.

    a. If you could do anything in life and money wasn't a factor what would it be?

    b. What could you see yourself doing if the impossible were possible?

    c. What does your life look like 10 years from now? Describe the picture.

    d. What would you do if you were absolutely fearless?

    e. What would you be doing if no one else had an opinion about it?

3. What group of people are you most affected by?

Each one of us has an audience we speak to. This is your sphere of influence. You do not have to be a professional with a platform to have a core group of people you affect the most. Many people believe they can only make a difference if they are speaking to a large group; however there are plenty of people who have been called to an audience of one. To help you recognize who this group is for your own life, ask yourself these questions:

    a. Who gives you purpose and makes you feel passionate? For some people its children, for others it's the elderly, maybe it's animals, entrepreneurs, teenagers.

    b. Do you know who most affects you?

    c. Who does your heart hurt and ache for?

    d. Who can bring you to tears?

    e. Who makes you want to do something to step up and help?

    f. Take some time to think about who your audience is and what your desire is to help them, speak to them and reach them.

Part 2

Creating Your Dream Pattern: The Principles Of A Dream

Chapter 7
Starting with the Z

Life can only be understood backwards,
but it must be lived forwards.
~Soren Kierkegaard

What if you lived your life backwards, knowing the end at the beginning, seeing all of your dreams come true, way bigger and better than you could have ever imagined? What if everything you have ever dreamt about happened with such tremendous success, played out perfectly, with every problem you've ever faced solved in the end? If that were the case, would you dream differently? Would you have more faith? Would you move in a forward direction with such fervor and joy knowing that nothing and no one could stop you? If every fear was removed and you knew that living your dream would become your reality and that you would succeed beyond your wildest imagination, would you do things differently? I believe there is tremendous power in seeing yourself at the end of your life, or as I call it at the 'Z'. It's in that place that your Creator has designed for you to end up, rather than in the current state of how you are living your life right now. I believe that by visualizing yourself there at the Z, as if all of your dreams have all come true, you could make them become a reality. If you can imagine the big picture and work backwards from that point, nothing can stop you! By working backwards as if all of your dreams came true, you would always believe, never doubt, always trust, and leave fear and worry behind for good because it was all a guaranteed win!

You see, your Creator has already designed your entire life out like a movie, knowing the end of your story at the beginning. That's a pretty powerful concept to grasp I know, but I can say that I've experienced this firsthand when living out a couple of my dreams, for example, when I launched my own magazine, *Boho.* Before creating it, I had visualized in my head how it would look and feel. What blew me away is that the very picture I was imagining came true and manifested before my eyes. From that day forward I recognized the principle, *if I could see it and believe it,* I could have it! It wasn't magic, it was divine intervention! I had possessed enough faith to *know* that the dream inside my heart wasn't just my crazy imagination, rather it was a vision planted there from my Creator. He gives us the picture, and then we have to get out the brushes and bring the painting to life! The reason God give us a picture is so that, during times of testing, trials and adversity, we have something to hold on to as a promise that the dream will come to pass.

I really love the story of Joseph. It's an excellent example of how God shows us the 'Z' (the end) at the beginning of our life. God put a dream in Joseph's heart that he would one day rule a nation and live a very victorious life. Joseph had a pure, unselfish heart and never desired to be in charge of anyone, but God had other plans. While Joseph was his father's favorite child, his brothers were very jealous of him and they ended up selling him into slavery. Joseph was also thrown in jail for many years for a crime he never committed. Yet, in spite of these harsh trials, instead of quitting on the dream God gave him, Joseph used these hard times as stepping-stones. God showed Joseph a prophetic picture of the Z at the beginning of his life because He knew Joseph would spend the first years of his life living completely contradictory to his dream. God's dream revealed to Joseph his destiny and true identity so that during these times of testing and trials he wouldn't give up or quit. Joseph was given a picture of his future. *God worked backwards.* At the beginning of Joseph's life, God showed him the END.

Today, I encourage you to live your life backwards, seeing the end of your life at the beginning, because that's how your Creator sees it and sees you. Believe in all of the dreams you are imagining, because they are God-given and planted. All you need to do is have the faith to believe in them.

TASK: Write down how your life looks at the end, the *Z,* in the fulfillment of all of your dreams, as if they all came true as big and grand as you can possibly imagine. Write it all down as if NOTHING was impossible. Most importantly, HAVE FUN doing this! If you can truly visualize in your heart every dream in all it's glory you have no idea how that will literally change the way you work towards actually seeing it happen in reality! You also can never imagine how much *more* your Creator will do beyond what you can see!

Chapter 8
Write Your Dream Vision Down

Dreaming, after all, is a form of planning.
~Gloria Steinem

Just like designing a dress, no dream can exist without a plan. Your first step in designing your dream is to create a detailed pattern before you can construct the real thing. Like designing a dress, while the ultimate goal is for the dress to be made and sold, it cannot be put into production before hundreds of planning steps take place first. To start the process of making the dress, the designer must first sketch it out on paper and then scan it into a computer to create a pattern. Next, it will be printed out and constructed into a paper pattern so that it can be molded onto a bustform to see if its measurements are accurate and work out all of the kinks. After that, the same steps are repeated and practiced with a muslin cloth. Then, finally, if all of the plans work out on paper and in the muslin, the garment can be made with fabric and sewn together to create the actual dress. It's the same with a dream. You have to plan out your pattern first, and try it out a couple of times before you can begin the construction of what you ultimately want to build.

Just because you plan for your dream doesn't make it less *dreamy.* One of the keys to seeing your dream come true is creating the strategy. Yes, you can have a winning idea, a supernatural talent, a grand vision, but if you don't take the time to write it all down and create a game plan for success, your dream is nothing more than just an idea floating in space. Success must be planned for; as Benjamin Franklin said, *"If you fail to plan, you are planning to fail."* You must plan, and write down your dream in detail. Now that may sound foreign or even uncomfortable for you to hear, especially if you are a dreamer by nature. But planning doesn't take away the dreamy part, nor does it take away from a free-spirited nature. Instead it empowers you to see your dreams come true and live them out. I remember back in the early stages of designing my own dreams that I wasn't exactly convinced about the importance of the planning part. I held tight to the belief that if things were 'meant to be' they would just happen, and I wouldn't have to do anything. I pretty much downplayed the entire process of planning, viewing it as a sign of being a control-freak and not being true to myself as the free-spirit I naturally was. I couldn't have been more wrong. What I discovered was that the success of living out my dream lay in the BALANCE of me both trusting in my faith and taking the first steps toward a plan of action! Just as an architect is hired to draw up plans before a house can be built and the foundation is poured, likewise, you must create a plan that will precisely outline the strategy to your dreams becoming a reality.

Dreams provide vision for your future.
If you don't have a dream in front of you as a place of vision, you will always look back to your past and do what you've done before. You will always assume what's happened before is what will happen in your future, and return to your comfort zone! Dreams provide vision for your future. They are magnets that pull you into your destiny. It's essential to look towards your future and keep your eyes ahead of you through the windshield of life, no longer through the rear view mirror. As Alan Lakein says, "Planning brings the future into the present so that you can do something about it now! "By taking the time to plan your dreams it will keep you in the present moving into your future.

So how do you start?

Sometimes the hardest step to take is the first one. Your dream will start off in the right direction if you take the first step of writing down what your vision looks like, and create a clear plan to see it through. I like how it's said in the book of *Habakkuk*: *"Write the vision down. Make it plain on tablets, that he may run who reads it. For the vision is for an appointed time, but at the end it will speak, and it will not lie. Though it tarries, wait for it; because it will surely come, it will not tarry."* To begin writing it down, start with a creative free-form brainstorming session where you put all of your ideas on paper.

Start with seeing yourself at the *Z*; as I mentioned in the previous chapter, write down all of your ideas, concepts, thoughts, *EVERYTHING*, even if the dots don't connect or make complete sense to you just yet. Allow yourself the openness of this exercise to just let your brain be free and release your dreams onto paper (or your electronic device). You have to start with the foundation before you can build the dream. If you sit down and take the time to build a strong plan for your dream you will be amazed how all of the details will begin to flesh themselves out, every little special idea in your mind will suddenly come flooding back to you. Don't miss this awesome opportunity to custom create everything you can ever imagine!

By creating a plan, you are proving on paper it's practical and attainable. As you put together the plan, don't be put off by the first couple of drafts being messy or imperfect, or even changing and transforming as you write. The entire idea behind the plan is to see what's missing, what's needed, etc. This is where you will begin to ask yourself questions, see holes, and possibly even reconsider some of your original ideas. During this process a lot of new questions may arise about your plan and I want to assure you that it's ok to change your plan. Don't be discouraged if everything on paper suddenly seems more complex or appears differently once you have written it out. Also, don't become overwhelmed because now you suddenly see all of these details in front of you. The purpose of a plan is to minimize the overwhelming feelings and move into creating such a well thought-out and detailed plan that all of those thoughts will leave your mind and end up on paper, just like a roadmap. Anyone who picks up the map (your dream plan) should be able to read it so plainly they can figure out which direction to go without you having to explain a word. The goal of creating this plan is to allow you to think through the entire dream as thoroughly as possible, building the best foundation for success, and get you to start doing what you have planned!

Chapter 9
Stop Daydreaming, Start Doing

If you can dream it, you can do it.
~Walt Disney

Lots of people have dreams, but dreaming without doing is called *daydreaming*, its dreaming without movement and corresponding action. Some people have dreams but they aren't willing to take the first step. Some aren't willing to sacrifice and do the hard work it takes to do them, but *dreams don't just happen*! Living your dream requires you taking practical action steps of hard work, discipline, sacrifice and perseverance. You have to invest the time and energy that your dream requires. Everything from training, internships, classes, mentoring, reading, researching and most of all real-life experiences are all part of the process you will need to walk through before the dream comes true. It takes the *'DO'* to see a dream come true!

Dreams don't manifest without action.
Daydreaming in your head all day long, brainstorming with friends, or talking about what you *plan* on doing is not the same as doing it! You cannot just wish and hope your dreams will magically come true some day. Your dreams will not come true unless you take the time to do what's required of you. There are so many people who have great ideas, yet they don't possess the passion or drive that will take them from ideas into action. If you have a great dream then do something about it. Commit to starting your dream and following through on it,

taking it from just words into the real world. It is always better to start something and have it evolve and change, than to never start anything at all.

Great things are done by a series of small things brought together. So says the artist Vincent van Gogh. It's not what you do once, but what you do over and over again that makes a dream happen. I didn't achieve my dream of creating my own sustainable fashion magazine or becoming a celebrity stylist for *O, the Oprah magazine* or even attending FIT by doing one great thing. I did it by doing a series of many, many, *many* SMALL actions that helped me lead up to it. This is truly how ideas translate into actions, and dreams become realities. It's those small, day-to-day, repeated actions that ultimately bring you to the place of success. That's not always the popular answer, as not everyone is interested in doing the hard work or consistent action that it takes to complete something. But I can promise you that if you take this approach to living, you will see your dreams fulfilled.

We live in a society today where we have become accustomed to the quick fix, but dreams don't play by those rules. What are truly required to see a dream come to pass are repeated actions of discipline. For a lot of people discipline is a dirty word. I just love how motivational speaker Jim Rohn explains the benefits of discipline "We must all suffer one of two things: the pain of discipline or the pain of disappointment." It's the truth! The idea of working hard past the pain and repeating the actions over and over again until you see the results doesn't bring a smile to many faces. But what would bring even more sadness would be the foolishness of not following discipline through, and ending up with the disappointment of never doing what you started. The interesting thing about being disciplined is that it's somehow viewed as a negative, feeling restrictive and like bondage. However, discipline is just the opposite, it's a positive. If you view discipline as the "bridge between goals and accomplishment" as Rohn puts it, you will see that the art of discipline will bring you to your dream, which is exactly the destination you want to end up at.

Good intentions vs. living intentionally.

One day I woke up and the word INTENTIONAL came to my heart. I started to think, was I being intentional about living the dream life I imagined in my head and what was I doing to move towards the direction in which I wanted to go? You see, you can have good intentions and mean to do something, yet never actually do it, or you can live intentionally and do things on purpose, letting your actions back up your words. Do you see the difference? I think it's so important to evaluate our lives and maintain our right to live with intention. This is a reward unto ourselves, because the payoff is so huge if we can follow through on what we say we are going to do. I am amazed how this little word can have so much weight. When you live intentionally, and do something on purpose, with the purpose of seeing it materialize, you can guarantee yourself a positive and fruitful outcome, especially when you become intentional about going after your dreams. If you do not make your dreams your focus, or purposely place what is important to you in front of you, your focus will always be somewhere else. You must every day remain steadfast, keeping your eye on the prize. You must be intentional. You see dreams will never happen by working just on a whim, without intention or focus. You must always keep your attention on what's in front of you, lest you turn back to the familiar, the comfort zone, and let time fly away. You can have good intentions, you can mean to work on your dream, but life will always get in the way. You cannot reach the goal, cross the finish line, or make it to the end of your dream if you are not willing to do whatever it takes to stay focused and intentional on every task that is needed to get you there. Nobody ever lived their dream by having good intentions. It was their actions that led them to move and go after their dreams intentionally that got them there.

Chapter 10
It Takes Teamwork
To Make A Dream Work

*Teamwork makes the dream work, but a vision
becomes a nightmare when the leader has a big
dream and a bad team.*
~ *John C. Maxwell*

You cannot achieve your dream without a team. While in the beginning you may be dreaming of the idea alone, there is no way humanly possible that a dream can be accomplished on your own without the help of others. From personal to professional, there will always be people sent along the way to assist you to get to where you need to go. Each person will bring their own contribution to what you're doing, so you need to be sure to appreciate those who have put in all of the love and support to help you make your dream come true. One of the lessons I've learned throughout this journey is that it's important to honor and value each person working with you, because you never know when these people will transition out of your life and move on. I can remember when I first started going after my dream, I had this naïve belief that everyone who started with me was also going to finish, but that was not the case. I learned that people will move in and out of your life for various reasons and seasons, and you can never predict when they will come in and when they will leave. When people come on board, it's essential that you understand this principle. If you can grasp this then you will be very successful at understanding the roles each person plays during your dream, without feeling hurt when it's time for them to exit.

Another misconception of having a dream team is thinking that everyone who works for you must possess the same skillset and function in the same gifts as you. This couldn't be further from the truth, and could be your biggest downfall if you believe so. Being a great team leader requires that you can identify what's missing in your own toolbox of skills and recognize these traits in others. Like a puzzle, everyone is his or her own special, uniquely shaped piece. If you want to put the puzzle together then you must have all of the different pieces and not multiples of the same pieces. Be sure to think of this parable when assembling your dream team. I've put together a list of the dream teams that I believe may play a part in your dream during one season or another. I believe this will help you identify the players.

The Cheerleading Squad: These are the people who will rally alongside of you when your dream is in its infant stages and during the challenges. They believe in you no matter what, and consistently help push you through whatever is needed at the time. They typically cheer you on with encouraging words, small gestures or emotional support. Everyone and anyone included in this group can be —but are not limited to—mentors, close friends, family, colleagues, and sometimes even distant social media acquaintances. Keep an open ear for people like this who believe in what you are doing before they ever see the fruits of your labor. You can never grasp the priceless value of these tokens of appreciation until the day comes when they are no longer there.

Family & Friends: These are the core people who will support you in various ways (typically for free most of the time!) and who will be the constant along your journey. Whether it's a grandmother offering to take care of your kids, a brother helping you pack up boxes filled with your newest product to ship it out before you can afford a production facility, or a friend who stays up all night with you putting the finishing touches on what you need to launch, these are the key players who will be there to assist you in whatever you need done at the time. Friends and family are typically the original seed planters in your dream. I want to encourage you to never take these people for granted simply because they are always there for you. These are your 'go to' team members and even though they are closest to you, you should never expect them to be.

The Worker Bees: If you are launching something new, you will definitely need a team of people who will be committed to working for you who are reliable and action oriented. You cannot accomplishyourdreamwithoutthem!Eventheonesvolunteeringtodothe smallest jobs like making photocopies, or running errands, these people can help tremendously in doing this kind of work so that you can focus on what you do best.

The Financiers: There may be some circumstances where you will need to have some significant funding to launch your dream. You may be the one with the idea, but there will be others who believe in your vision and want to come alongside of you and support your dream financially. These people will probably make you think very much outside your comfort zone and challenge you to see things differently, but don't despise it. Allow their wisdom to help grow your thinking and take your dream to a new level.

When creating your dream team choose your players wisely. Everyone who wants to play should appreciate and share your vision, desiring to support you in succeeding. They are there to support your dream, and not attempt to create their own, or bring negative energy in that would take away from it. Never let anyone on your team who has a critical spirit. Always trust your instincts when it comes to people; even if they beg you to be on your team, if your inner compass says "no" then don't let them be. All players should bring flavor and life to your dream, and help make it come true. They should be there to help you move towards your goal. There is no room to settle for less than the best.

Chapter 11
Mentors Make All The Difference

Walk with the dreamers, the believers, the courageous, the cheerful, the planners, the doers, the successful people with their head in the clouds and their feet on the ground. Let their spirit ignite a fire within you to leave this world better than when you found it.

~Wilfred Peterson

There will be plenty of opportunities to push through the dream process alone, but the people in your life who will become your mentors will give you big breaks and take a chance on you. It's those people who will play an integral role in helping you achieve your dream. When someone is wiser, more experienced and better equipped in an area than you are, and they are willing to share that wisdom with you, you must embrace it with everything in you, and soak in all they have to offer. Mentors will challenge you to go higher. They will bring wisdom and opportunity to you. Do not try to compete with them, you never will. Instead, honor and value them for them paving the way before you. For if they never created that path, you would never have the opportunity to one day walk it yourself. A mentor helps prepare you for your dream. They are invaluable to your dream journey because in many ways they escort you into it. My recommendation is to seek out a mentor for every area of your life. A career mentor, a spiritual mentor, a relationship mentor, a parenting mentor, etc.; different mentors serve different purposes. Mentors also help keep you accountable to stay on the right path. Like a shepherd, they will correct you if they see you starting to head off course, but they will do so in love because they want what's best for you. Mentors will help train you for living your dreams, and will be an example of what they look like in reality! Here is a glimpse into two of my most favorite mentors in my career. I think they both stand out as excellent examples of what a successful mentor looks like.

Mentor #1 Dee, The Gap

I can recall my first mentor when I was only 16 years old. I was still in high school and landed my very first fashion job at the Gap in the Ocean County Mall. My parents agreed to drive me back and forth while I worked nights and weekends after school. Once I was hired I met the staff and one very special person made an impression on me, her name was Dee. She was tall, blonde, and powerful, everything that I wasn't. She towered over me both in height and stature. She had been a seasoned veteran with the company in a position at that time I could only dream of. She was in charge of everyone, but never let anyone feel like they were beneath her. She was full of acceptance for people, yet had a diligence for running the business at the same time. I sooo wanted to be in her shoes in every way! Because this was my very first job in fashion, I pretty much wanted to 'make it known' that my only goal was to become a huge success in New York City working in the fashion industry. Somehow I believed this was my road to get there, and I told Dee that I was willing to do whatever it took to make it happen—fold clothes, steam, iron, mop the floor, you name it, I would do it! At the time I was so hungry to learn everything and anything about the fashion industry and how it worked. I truly believed that if I could convince Dee that I was worth investing in, she would teach me everything she knew! Well, It didn't take long before Dee took notice of me, probably because I was relentless at running my mouth about my passion for working in fashion. I'm sure she got tired of hearing me beg for her wisdom, and for her blessing at giving me a chance to dress the windows, but I believed it was because she saw my fiery passion for succeeding that she eventually agreed to pour into me and become a mentor. You see Dee taught me that changing the fashion world started by doing odd tasks that nobody else wanted to do. Those jobs were typical retail sales stuff like folding and refolding clothes until 10pm every night, putting tickets back on returned merchandise, being friendly to people you didn't know or who were mean to you for no reason, helping style people's looks by giving them honest advice, not just phony conversation to get a sale, sweeping & mopping the floor and even cleaning the bathrooms, all done with a *GREAT POSITIVE ATTITUDE!* Wow, not exactly what I had dreamed working for a fashion retailer would be like, but Dee said the only way to get to the top was to start at the bottom. So I decided to heed her advice, and for that year, in exchange for me working in sales and dressing an occasional bust form, Dee poured into me everything she knew about working and managing business for a big branded retailer like Gap. At that time the Gap was the #1 fashion chain in the country, so to be exposed to this wisdom was priceless. Over time, Dee became a trusted friend and valued mentor. She always encouraged me to push myself harder, and demonstrate both integrity and character while doing even the most mundane tasks. She instilled into me a sense of acceptance for others who were different than me, which became an invaluable tool for attending fashion school and eventually living in New York City. She had the best laugh ever, and taught me the value of humor that helped those long retail days and nights go by fast. But most importantly, she showed me that above all else, when you are working for another company, you must ALWAYS treat that company as though it were your own. There were no shortcuts to success. Today, Dee has spent more than 25 years running some of the most successful retailers in the country.

Mentor #2- Shannon, Nordstrom

A few years later, when I was working for Nordstrom, another mentor opportunity came along. I noticed that the 'tall, strong blonde' became a theme of mine when it came to mentors. It wasn't purposeful, however perhaps a bit subconscious that I looked up to these women in positions whose shoes I so wanted to fill. They were both extremely passionate and powerful women who were at the top of their game, gifted in both creativity and business. Yes, they may have looked physically the opposite of me, but what they represented was everything I wanted to be in my career. They each represented the REALITY of my dream. I wanted to be them in a sense, when I 'made it'. It was like seeing my dream live and in action every day, with living proof that it was, in fact, POSSIBLE for me to get there one day. That reality of someone who was living my dream leads me to the introduction of my most influential mentor, Shannon. Shannon was a west-coaster, who hailed from Seattle. Her career focus was sharper than a laser gun, and she had thicker skin than any New Yorker I'd ever met (despite her not being a NY native). She was beautiful, brilliant, extremely quick-on-her feet, and undeniably strong-willed. She was a creative powerhouse that pushed everyone who worked for her to their creative limits, making sure that every ounce of what you were capable of was being used to its maximum potential. I, as well as everyone else who worked for her, considered her to be our own Martha Stewart. Not only did she have a very close resemblance to her physical appearance, but also her talents were unmatched and she accepted *NOTHING* short of perfection if you worked for her.

At the time I was working for Nordstrom as a Fashion Stylist, Shannon was my Regional Manager. Everyone knew her tough cookie personality. She was extremely short on compliments, and people pretty much feared her. She was fiery, but I loved it! I found it an exciting challenge to prove to her I had 'it'. Despite the fact that everyone told me she "never gives compliments" and to remove my rose-colored glasses, that woman gave me the biggest compliment of my career, and it stuck with me ever since. This very statement she spoke to me propelled me to pursue my passion. It was after a long, exhausting day of work and all I can recall is her turning around, looking me straight in the eyes (I feared I was getting in trouble!) and saying to me, *"You, my dear, have a fire in your belly!"* followed up by… *"and you'd better follow it!"* What? How did she see that in me? She actually saw the passion inside of me that I was trying to prove throughout my entire career in fashion? At that moment, I felt like she saw herself in me, which was the hugest compliment for this 25-year-old! In my career, to have your talents recognized by someone in a regional position, who was hardly ever impressed, was an absolute honor! Because I had valued her opinion and the fact that she saw something special in me, from that day forward I vowed to make sure I soaked up every ounce of wisdom she had (good or bad). I worked extremely hard, sacrificing a ton to prove to Shannon that she was right about me! I never, ever wanted to let her down or let her see me fail to do any less than my best!

After that, I was quickly promoted in 3 short months to a Visual Manager with my own store in New York, and then only 3 months later promoted again, to become the Regional Fashion Stylist for the North East region of Nordstrom. At that time I felt, because of Shannon's support, belief and fanning of the flame within me, that this was what helped me to never quit and keep pursuing my dreams. Working this position in my 20's was my ultimate dream job. I was styling and producing fashion shows in conjunction with top magazines like *Vogue, Harper's Bazaar, and InStyle* to benefit world-changing charities, and styling clothes from the most famous designers like *Armani, Dolce & Gabbana, Versace, Gucci, and Prada,* the best of the best! I got to see fashion collections before anyone else, and have clothes flown in directly from the fashion houses in Paris and Milan. It was the ultimate fashion stylist's dream. I enjoyed a nice salary to play with the best fashion in the world, and got to style for hours and hours and hours! I learned how to produce my own fashion shows, create my own storyboards, select the models, design and choose hair and makeup teams, music, lighting, and staging, all of it! I produced live fashion shows for up to 500 people in attendance with sometimes 30 plus models in a show, styling every one of them head to toe, with my vision! It was literally my most favorite corporate job of my fashion career! If it hadn't been for Shannon taking an interest in me, sacrificing her valuable time to teach me, and giving me a chance to prove myself because she saw the talent in me, I don't believe I would have ever had this experience of living one of my dreams.

Today, Shannon is a Director for Starbucks. She lives in her dream home on an island in Seattle and is truly living out everything she's imagined. She's a living testament that if you stay focused, work your tail off, and never ever relent, you will see your dreams come true!

Chapter 12
Financing Your Dream

Making money is art, working is art and
good business is the best art.
~Andy Warhol

It is said that where there is vision, there will be provision. However, if you plan on starting your own business, launching a brand, creating a charity, or whatever your dream is, you will always have to spend the time creating a well thought-out financial plan to manage that provision properly. I'm not speaking about a business plan, but rather, in addition to that, I am talking about creating a detailed financial plan that outlines every aspect of your dream's finances and goals. I always like to ask someone who tells me that they are ready to live their dream this question; "If I hand you a check for a million dollars right now, how would you spend it?" I ask this question because their answer tells me whether or not they are truly prepared for their dream. To see your dream happen, you must have a financial plan on paper, in detail, of how you would handle the money. You should be planning with the mindset that you already have the money in your hands, before you actually receive it.

I have seen many dreamers fail because of their lack of attention to or interest in financial planning. I've also seen many people driven more by their passion and what makes them feel emotionally fulfilled, over a drive for financial success. On the upside, it is our passion that fuels the fire, but sometimes it's what also gets us burned. Sometimes we can be so close to our dreams that it's hard to separate the passion for them with the practical knowledge of wanting to deal with the finances of them. When this happens, we tend not to be as successful at propelling our dream forward because we are too personally attached to our idea. This can be the downfall of your dream if you don't understand how to separate your passion for your idea from the practically of a profit and loss statement. The saying is true, "If you fail to plan, you plan to fail," and, like it or not, creating a sound financial plan for your dream is a key to its success. Some of you may have to quit your job to start your dream, or you may have to work a freelance job or part-time in order to begin your dream. If you haven't planned on how to manage your money in order for you to finance your way into a dream, then you must make it a priority and not run away from this seemingly uncreative or intimidating part of the process.

I can remember when I first launched one of my big dreams I was wearing rose-colored glasses regarding my financial plan. I knew that I should always be knowledgeable of every aspect of my business, but the number crunching gave me anxiety. For some reason, I had a fear of making mistakes and not being perfectly accurate. Like most young entrepreneurs, I also didn't have my entire money making plan perfectly figured out, so that also frustrated me. It wasn't until one day I was asked by a close friend who worked on Wall Street to see my financial plan that I even realized my current business plan didn't include enough financial details. Yes, I had created a very strong, detailed and laid out business plan with goal projections and realistic numbers, but the down and dirty fiscal details someone who was going to loan me money was looking for were lacking. It was a tough lesson to learn that running from my fear of being imperfect would actually hurt me in the end. Instead, I should have faced my fear of imperfection and asked for help. I realized that day that, while I may not be able to be the expert in every area of my business, I could find the right person who would be, and learn from them. The only way to ever see your dream come alive is to first see it on paper in black and white. Then, will you be prepared to receive your dream.

You are not selling out just because you are paying attention to money.

I have had a lot of people share with me, especially those who are *dreamier* by nature, that they believe that talking about money removes the authenticity away from their creative ideas. It's as if they believe that if you pay attention to money, then you are suddenly no longer an artist, like you are 'selling out'. But this couldn't be further from the truth. You need to have a healthy relationship with money in order to get your finances in the place where you can actually see your dreams come true, and stop just dreaming about them! If you stay in the place of being idealistic, sticking to the concept that money doesn't matter, then you will never see your dream get off the ground. Money is a tool. Without money you can't feed a nation, build a water-well, save children from sex trafficking, or get anything done! You must become more intelligent about money, and view money as a means to an end, not as a chain that holds you back from your dreamy, idealistic nature. You can control money and how you use it, and not let it control you. You can take authority over your money and use it for good and not evil. Money by itself is not evil; rather it is the love of money, being so in love with it that you become selfish, greedy and addicted to having it, that makes it a bad thing. It's a dangerous place to live, believing this misconception of money. I challenge you to put aside these negative beliefs and begin to develop a solid relationship with money so that you can launch your dream! If you struggle with doing it alone, I recommend finding a financial planner who can help you set your goals and work towards your dream. These people are experts in helping with both the short-term and long-term planning of your dreams. Even our *Boho Dream Academy* offers classes with Financial Planners to help you get started, which you can find on my website, GinaLaMorte.com. I'm truly excited for you to get comfortable with this part of planning your dream, as I know it will help you see your dreams come true.

Investing in your dream doesn't mean only finances.

While we can never know the precise timing of a dream, what we can know is that timing involves seasons, and seasons consist of the principle of sowing and reaping. When it comes to dreams you have got to do quite a bit of sowing, in many areas, before it's time for your dream to bloom. It could be years before you see that dream harvest. However, the law of sowing and reaping is definitive, so if you spend your time and money investing in your dream, and investing in the dreams of others, you can bank on your dream seed blossoming one day into a strong, towering tree with deep roots. Think about what seeds you need in order to see your dream come into harvest. Take some time to look at everything it's going to take and start sowing into someone else's dream what you need. This means if you need finances for your dream, give money to support someone else's dream. If you need support in building a website, offer to help someone else in that same area. What you sow into others comes back to you in a harvest, so be generous and don't be afraid to sow. Even if you have planted seeds years ago and you think they've died, you're wrong. No seed sown is ever dead, only buried. There's always an incubation period, time to be watered, and then a ground breaking to meet the sun. I like this proverb found in Galatians 6:9 as a reminder. It says, "Don't get tired of helping others. You will be rewarded when the time is right, if you don't give up." Timing is everything. Don't miss the opportunity to invest in your own dream by planting seeds in someone else's. You will never come up without a harvest, for in due time you will reap what you have sown.

Part Three

From Concept to Creation: The Journey of A Dream

Chapter 13
Crawl Before You Fly

Even though we are benched for a season does not mean
we don't show up to practice and get prepared to play.
There will be a time when the coach calls us up to bat.
~ Gentry Lane

Sometimes it seems nearly impossible to get excited about your dreams when you feel like the caterpillar and not the butterfly. When you are still in the caterpillar stage it can be painful, confusing and exhausting. When you have no wings and you are crawling on the floor it's not easy to remember that your guaranteed outcome is becoming that of a beautiful, colorful butterfly. The majority of your dream is spent in the cocoon. It's dark and uncomfortable. The more you grow, the more you want to get out and fly, but you can only fly when your wings are ready. It takes time to grow and develop inside of the cocoon. It is absolutely frustrating knowing you have this thing inside of you waiting to be birthed, yet it's not time.

The majority of your dream journey is spent growing, learning, and ultimately preparing you to become the person that you will need to be in order to live out your dream. In these dark times it's easy to get discouraged and think your dreams are never going to happen, when it's quite the opposite. It's in these times that your dreams are getting you prepared for what is about to happen. Your character is being formed during this time of stretching. You are being trained to do exactly what you are dreaming of doing, but it happens while you are doing the most mundane of seemingly unrelated tasks (think *The Karate Kid* "Wax on. Wax off.") So while during this time you wish your dreams would hurry up and happen, it's much better to get your character flaws and attitude adjustments worked out in the dark, while no one is watching. While waiting in this cocoon you develop patience, perseverance, and a deeper prayer life. You become more in tune with your Creator. You learn to press through the hard times even when you don't want to, and gain the faith experience to know that if you see things through you will see your dreams come true.

Another wonderful illustration to help you understand the journey of a dream is to compare it to birthing a baby. You will have the dream seed planted in you and you will be so excited but you can't see any outward signs. Then you will start seeing glimpses of what looks to be a baby, yet there are still many months before the baby will be born. People start giving their opinions on names that you don't like. You start feeling really uncomfortable, nothing fits, and you begin to wonder if you can handle all of it. Eventually, you become so tired and irritable that you just want to push the baby out before it's time. Finally, the day of its birth arrives and there is incredible pain beyond comprehension and you really don't think you will survive, until something or someone comes along to give you a little relief. It's one last major push and out comes the most beautiful baby you've ever seen in your life! You cry for joy because you could never have imagined something so beautiful and in an instant all of the pain is gone and there's nothing but elation! The baby has arrived! Yes, birthing a dream is like that! So, just as you won't want to have the baby prematurely, you don't want to give up on birthing your dream. Ultimately, there is joy in the pain of going through the process of making it full term. It's all about what you choose to focus on, and understanding in the end that it's all worth it!

Testing and trials.

I have learned through my experience of waiting for a dream to manifest that when you are first given the vision for your dream it will be a very exciting time of creativity and inspiration. You will have so much fiery passion that you will throw yourself into doing whatever you can to start designing that dream. However, the next season following that positive groove will be a time of testing. Your dream will be so tested that everything and everyone will come up against you, challenging you about whether you truly believe your dream will actually become a reality. It will be a time when reasoning steps in and it will become very hard to believe in your dreams when you are living in the place where everything looks opposite to what you believe to be true. It will be the biggest test of your faith when you may not have the money, time, or even talent to accomplish the dream that is in your heart, yet you still pursue it. You have got to believe in your dream so much that, no matter what anyone else tells you, no matter how impossible your circumstances appear, you never stop believing in what you are called to do until you see it manifest. This testing time between having the vision for your dream and ultimately experiencing it can seem like a long, dark journey, but be encouraged, for your outcome will be the beautiful butterfly as long as you don't quit.

What you are full of will come out before your dream shows up.
Do you know what you are full of? When you breakdown compound words that you can relate to and define you, then you can see what is going on inside of you. Are you *Care-ful – consumed with cares? Fear-ful – filled with fear? Joy-ful – full of joy? Beauti-ful – full of beauty?* What is consuming your mind, body and spirit, trying to break it down and take you down? These words that you believe you are full of can make or break a dream. I want you to meditate on some of these words you may think describe you best. Once you recognize them, if you notice they tend to be more negative, then allow yourself to find more positive *FULL* words that can *FILL* you up instead of deplete your tank.

Chapter 14
Trusting Your Inner Compass

*Instinct is a marvelous thing. It can neither be
explained nor ignored.*
~ Agatha Christie

Howard Schultz of Starbucks went from living in the housing projects of Canarsie, Brooklyn to building Starbucks into a $56 billion dollar company. His mother didn't believe in him when he started the job and asked him, "Who's going to buy coffee?" Can you imagine? His own mother couldn't see the vision he had. If we listen to the unbelieving voices in our lives instead of our own inner compass, we may miss out on some of our biggest dreams. If Howard had heeded his mother's doubting voice instead of following what he believed intuitively, he may never have gotten out of the projects and built one of the most successfully branded businesses, literally changing the way we experience coffee today. Life throws us many opportunities to doubt our dreams based on what others have to say about them. In fact, one of the biggest lessons to learn is how to tune out these voices and tune into your own inner compass. Our inner compass is our guidepost. It provides truth and direction. It leads us into our destiny. If we follow it we can avoid lots of hurt and disappointment, and see our dreams become reality. You have to learn to trust yourself and your own vision. You have got to be willing to follow what's in your heart, even when others cannot see it. You also cannot get upset with other people who don't see your vision, because it's not theirs to see. There will be people who do not believe in your dream, like Schultz's own mother. You have to make the conscious choice to listen to your inner compass, even when the doubters come along.

Go with your gut.

There's a reason we call it a 'gut instinct'. It's described as that first 'feeling or impression' that we feel in our, well, gut. It's that still, small voice, that knowing in your heart, despite what your mind is rationalizing with you. I believe it is God speaking. I can't express to you enough how integral it is to your life to follow your *first* gut instinct, as opposed to the other voices that may be vying for your attention. Learning how to silence the outside noise takes practice, but if you start with small steps of following that inner knowing for the first time, you will soon see the positive results in your life. One thing I did learn that became invaluable to me was not condemning myself for making a wrong decision (if for some reason I didn't follow my inner compass). Everyone can get off track at one point or another, and if you do, please don't worry about it. You can always get back to exactly where you started by doing what a hiker does; simply turn around, and retrace your steps that lead you back to that starting point. It is never too late to begin again, but it's so worth it to train yourself to trust and follow the direction of that first *initial* impression and never discount it, *NO MATTER WHAT*.

Questioning your instincts

Even though I was a leader and a dreamer, for the earlier part of my life I was also a doubter. I constantly questioned whether or not my dreams were based in reality or if I simply wanted to escape it. It is a fact that in the early years of dreaming, before you gain the experience of living one out, you will constantly be questioning yourself if all of these visions you have are true or if you have just lost your mind! I could remember being bombarded with negative thoughts like "you are crazy, who are you to think your dreams will come true?" Especially because my dreams were quite big and unrealistic, at that time there was nothing tangible to lead me to believe my dreams were for real.

During those dark years of doubt, I would waver back and forth seeking the opinions of others over trusting my own instincts I assumed the false belief that someone else always knew more than me and was constantly second-guessing my choices. When you have big dreams you have to remember that along with those dreams comes the belief and faith in the impossible. You also have to be confident in the fact that you may be the only one who can see or catch that vision, so you will need to be able to make both large and small decisions. What I realized over time was that I was actually afraid to make the wrong decision. I had a fear of stepping out to accomplish my dreams and being wrong. Luckily, I had a mother who always assured me growing up that the God I served was bigger than any of my mistakes. She would say, "If you make a wrong decision so what? He's the Creator of the universe, I am pretty sure He can handle your misstep." Somehow that always settled me. The key to conquering this fear is to magnify your Creator and focus less on the embarrassment you'll face if you make the wrong choice. Then, and only then, will you develop the truth of following your own instincts.

Listen more, speak less.
My maternal grandfather was a man of few words. He was quietly confident, and quite reserved. I feared him, not in a bad way but in a "he doesn't say much, so when he does have something to say I better pay full attention" way. I'll never forget the day I was sitting in my grandparents' kitchen and I was jabbering away on what I thought, what I felt, blah, blah, blah ... like I knew it all. Then my Grandpa Joe decided to say one thing. "Kid, you'll learn more if you talk less and listen more. That's why you have two ears and one mouth." After that day, every business meeting I ever sat in, every person who could even possibly know more than me, I listened to. This was the best advice I could have gotten if I wanted to live my dreams. I learned a heck of a lot more listening to those who had wisdom and had gone before me

than hearing myself talk before I walked the walk!

This sage advice has stuck with me even till today. No matter whom I meet I allow them to speak and I listen to what they have to say. In *Proverbs* it says, "For out of the mouth, the heart speaks." It's amazing what you can learn just by listening.

Chapter 15
Size Doesn't Matter

The value of a dream has nothing to do with size, but rather the positive impact it can have on the life of someone else. There is a misconception that dreams are only worth pursuing if they are big, but that's not the case. Dreams, whether big or small, reaching one person or one million people, are all valued the same. Just like people, dreams come in all sizes and styles. To disregard a dream because on the surface it appears microscopic would be as to say a mustard seed has no value. Yet quite the opposite, a mustard seed yields the largest, most mighty standing tree. Next time you feel your dream is small, remind yourself of the mustard seed. You truly have no idea what that small seed will bloom into.

I can say that I have always dreamed big because it was just in my DNA. I tend to always see in a big vision, rather than in smaller parts. So the stretch for me comes in focusing on the granule, rather than visualizing the big picture. However, sometimes our minds cannot comprehend the vastness of a dream because we have a limited imagination. I believe that if you have a dream that looks impossible to you,then God actually has something designed for you that's even greater than you can imagine. I think th e quote from the *Passion Translation* book *Letters from Heaven* by Brian Simmons sums it up,

"Never doubt God's mighty power to work in you and accomplish all this. He will achieve infinitely more than your greatest request, your most unbelievable dream, and exceed your wildest imagination!" Those words confirm God gives you dreams, and wants to give you *even more* than you can ever imagine in your wildest imagination! Now that's a promise to hold on to!

Dreaming big.
If you want to dream bigger, then you have to get out of your tent and start looking at the stars. If you can gain an unlimited perspective, the dreams in your heart will begin to explode like fireworks inside of you. Then you will be able to soar to greater heights where your breathing may need some adjustments. Once you settle in that space, you will feel freer than you have ever felt. I know that my dreams are defined as seeing the world through a new lens, someone else's perspective, and a global view. Seeing life through just your own eyes is dull (at least I think so!); looking through another's lens, I believe, is what life is all about. I want to take every opportunity to see life the way someone else does. I may have traveled much already in my short lifetime, but I can't wait to spend the rest of my life exploring new places I've yet to see. I let my passion allow me to dream BIGGER, HIGHER and WILDER than my limited imagination. I want to soar to new, unlimited heights. For me, traveling the world, getting inspired by other cultures, engaging with new people who have different point of views than I do, that inspires me. I want to learn from them, see life through their eyes, and try to understand what it's like to walk in their shoes. I suddenly see the world is an unlimited place and discover that my binocular point of view is not the only way life exists. My passion for seeing how other people and cultures live inspires me to go to new levels and greater heights than my heart has ever gone before. I become ready to soar up to an altitude that takes me way out of my comfort zone and into a space where I need to adjust my breathing. So I ask you, where are your dreams leading you? Are they taking you outside of your comfort zone?

Being overwhelmed by a dream beyond your size.

How do you accomplish your dreams when they seem so big, and many times feel too overwhelming to accomplish? My answer? One day at a time. At times when your dream seems so much greater than you, you've got to take a step back and begin to learn the art of living one day at a time, even while you are planning for the future. Living in the moment is truly a present. If your future goal seems way too grand to grasp, shift your focus onto today. I can remember times in my life where things appeared so overwhelming to me that I could not even focus on the day, but rather could only focus on one hour at a time. It is your own journey so you should never feel guilty or like a failure if the big picture doesn't always come easy to you. Sometimes life just calls you to live right where you're at. I love this thought *"If you look down at your feet that is exactly where you are supposed to be right now."* So no matter what your dream, no matter how big it is, no matter how overwhelming it may feel at times, it's completely ok to simplify it all and just take it one day at a time.

Be willing to dream outside of your comfort zone.

One thing I have learned about dreams is that they only happen when you live outside of your comfort zone. As time goes by, we can get really comfortable, and the idea of doing something new to shake our safety net does not always feel so good. However, if you want to see your dreams come true, and see things you've never seen before, you need to do things you've never done before! To live out your dreams, you've got to be willing to step away from what feels comfortable and stretch yourself into new territory, no matter how awkward or scary it feels. Realize that feeling fear, trembling, or any kind of trepidation to walking out your dreams is natural, but no matter how uncomfortable it feels, be willing to dream outside of your comfort zone.

Chapter 16
Heredity Doesn't
Determine Destiny

There are two great days in a person's life;
the day we are born and the day we discover why.
~William Barclay

I love this phrase: "Don't ever downgrade your dream to fit your reality. Upgrade your conviction to match your destiny." So many people feel they don't come from the proper background in order to do what they dream. They think their current lifestyle defines who they are. They think, *Well, I wasn't raised in a family that encouraged me much,* or *I didn't come from a privileged background.* Sometimes we are part of family that has been in a cycle of defeat, was abusive, or financially lacking. Others may have come from families raised very rigidly, where practicality and facts took priority over dreams. Some of you may have no idea about the lineage of your roots and weren't raised to believe anything specific. The truth is, your heredity doesn't determine your destiny. When it comes to dreams, it's solely based on the God-given desires and gifts you were born with, and has nothing to do with the means by which you were raised. Yes, you will develop mindsets and thought patterns, morals and values from how you grew up, but, intuitively, at the end of the day you have your own voice, will and desire to determine which direction in life you will go.

What does help steer the direction of your dreams and make your path more or less of a challenge will be how your parents or parent (or guardian, family member) raised you, in the sense of what type of encouragement, or lack thereof, was going on in the household. Were you taught to believe in the impossible or were you led to believe the facts are the facts? My father used to tell me all the time while growing up, "Gina, you can be anything you want to be. That's what our country is all about. If you want to be the President, you can be. Just follow what's in your heart and always be true to yourself."

In college, my Dad would send me letters that were filled with some of his favorite inspirational quotes from poets like Emerson, Thoreau and Frost. His most beloved was by Alfred Lord Tennyson *"That which we are, we are; One equal temper of heroic hearts. Made weak by time and fate, but strong in will. To strive, to seek, to find, and not to yield."* They always stuck with me and kept me encouraged to keep pursuing my dreams, and to never *ever* give up on them. On the flip side, along my dream journey there were other people telling me that my dreams were unrealistic. Plenty of people shared their thoughts about how they didn't think an Italian girl from the shore of New Jersey, who was the first family member to attend college, could ever amount to much. How wrong they were!

When God gives you an assignment it doesn't matter who you are or where you come from. You don't have to possess the perfect qualifications. In fact, sometimes even the most excellent qualifications won't help you. So while who you are may be important for some, if you choose to follow the destiny dreams inside of you, all that matters is whose you are, a child of God with a kingdom connection. All other 'connections' need not be important.

Chapter 17
Your Test Becomes
Your Testimony

Lay a firm foundation with the bricks that
others throw at you.
~David Brinkley

The trials you have faced in the past will ultimately bring purpose to your pain. They will teach the tools of how to turn your test into your testimony, which, in turn, will help others along their journey too. I probably couldn't have written this chapter when I began writing this book. Mainly because before that I did not get to experience a true "test" that I would have to go through regarding my dream. As with any test, promotion is the reward for passing. I don't say this to scare you, but rather to alert you that along your dream journey there will be times when, out of nowhere, and I mean nowhere, a roadblock, or an all out war may come against you. No need for alarm; as with most dreams there will always be a Goliath in your path that you must conquer.

Think about it like this, the enemy of your soul does not want to see you succeed and make the world a better place by pursuing your dream. Therefore, anything that can be thrown your way to hurt you, disrupt you or damage you will try to come up against you. Your enemy hopes that if you can be knocked down enough, you will become this wounded person with lots of baggage. Baggage that becomes so heavy that you quit working towards your dream because you simply aren't strong enough to outlast it. But this is *NOT* the end of your story. This is simply a chapter in your book. These are just bricks with which to build your foundation. They are tools for your tool belt. If you can withstand all the daggers thrown at you and keep standing long enough until they stop coming at you, then you will reach your destination and see your dream come true! Ultimately, everything you learn during these tests will be part of your story and end up being used to help someone else who may one day face what you did.

Everything will work in your favor.
Let me tell you firmly that everything—and I do mean *EVERY-THING*—that you have learned, that you have been through, that you thought would kill you, will be used to your advantage to accomplish your dream. Those things that you felt were a waste of time; the hard times you thought would break you—when it's time for your dream to manifest in it's fulfillment you will utilize every skill you gained going through the tough times to actually propel you forward into living out your dream. It all ends up working in your favor! *ALL of it!*

   I remember working for a magazine as an editor for a couple of years. This magazine had an excellent circulation and was very successful. However, at one point they were extremely understaffed. That led me to running most of the editorial side of the publication by myself. At the time I was extremely frustrated and often stressed that I had to run the magazine alone, with little to no staff. While I was able to hire freelancers, it was honestly too much work for just one person. There were many moments when I complained and was completely annoyed about doing the entire editorial myself. It simply made no sense to me why I was going through this experience alone. What I didn't realize at the time was that it taught me how to do every single person's job, and literally gave me the education I needed later on to run my own magazine. It was in that moment I had realized that this once frustrating experience was actually my training in disguise. The lesson here is that you should never despise the moments in your life that seem to be challenging and make no sense. Instead, learn to embrace those moments and celebrate knowing that it's in those times that you are being trained and prepared for your dreams!

Don't let a chapter in your life be the entire story.

When you go through the tests and trials of life, you may feel pressured to stay in that place and believe that's your entire story. However, your setback was never meant to defeat you, it was meant to promote you. When you are going through tough times you won't see it that way, instead you will think that life won't get any better and that this is the end, but that's not the truth. It's only a chapter. I don't want you to waste your life or waste your talents because somebody hurt you and made you feel like you aren't important. Yes, plenty of bad things may have happened to you, but you cannot let the people or circumstances that tried to destroy you ruin the rest of your life. The storms of life can be heavy and frustrating at times, but these are chapters in your life, they are *NOT* the full story. I can only say from personal experience that if you press forward, even when you don't want to, even when it hurts, even when you have the worst attitude and everyone gets on your nerves, even when you think the world is against you, even when you have lost all hope, you *MUST* get back up and move ahead. If you do this, I promise that your life will turn into something great! It may not be perfect, it may not be in your timing, but it will be better than you have ever imagined in your head.

See yourself as the amazingly talented, beautiful, and brilliant person you are. You are not your circumstances that have happened to you. You were born with great talents that are there to help you have an amazing life, a life that can help others. Don't let a bad chapter be your entire story, and don't waste the talents God has given you. Even though the tough times were not God-sent, they will be God-used. So pull yourself out of that pit and start a new chapter. All of those tests will become your testimony if you allow them to be used to help other people who one day may be in the same place you once were. Nothing and no one can stop God's plan for your life. The bad times are just chapters. Turn the page. The end of your story is victorious!

Chapter 18
Failing Forward

Think like a Queen. A Queen is not afraid to fail.
Failure is another steppingstone to greatness.
~ Oprah Winfrey

Failing is not fun. In fact, it's like the last thing anyone ever wants to happen, and when it does you feel like it's the end of the road, and that you will never make it through, but I am here to tell you that you will! It's not like anyone sets out to fail on purpose. Seriously, can you imagine starting a dream and saying, "I can't wait to start and fail?" No! But the scariest part about failing isn't the failure itself; it's the anticipation leading up to the possibility of failing. For me, because I was a perfectionist at one point in my life, failure felt like death. It was never an option. I believed I would be less of a person if I failed, as if I wasn't on my best game. I didn't realize that I could fail at something and not be a failure. There was a difference. I probably made it much harder for myself because I was raised to always have a positive mentality, believing that there is a solution for everything. If I had a challenge, I believed that someway, somehow, I could face it head on and figure out a way to fix it! The reality of this is that it's simply not true. Sometimes you must fail at something to learn what not to do. It was a hard lesson for me to learn how to fail forward, and not sink deep into a depression because everything didn't always work out as I hoped or planned. Up until this point I had been quite blessed (so I thought!) not to have ever met failure, literally doing everything in my power to avoid it. Then it happened, or should I say life happened?

It was the day that I had pretty much dreaded my entire life, all of my dreams came crashing down around me. People, things, and situations—basically life had thrown me a curve ball. I didn't expect it. I couldn't have predicted it. No matter how much I had imagined or planned for all of the success in my life sometimes life just happens. It doesn't go how we plan, because life is NOT PERFECT. Why did I not realize this before? Why did I have to come face to face with things not working out the way I wanted? At that time I did not have the answers. All I had left was my faith and trust in God, which I realized was all I needed. Failing hurt like hell. I screamed, cried, and was sad for months. I questioned myself over and over and over, if I did something better could I have fixed it?

In the end I realized NOTHING I could have done would have changed the failure. In fact, once I bounced back from my depression and finally began to notice the sunlight again, I started kicking my own butt into gear and forced myself to start reading about other extremely successful businessmen and women who had also failed. Why didn't I do this sooner? It would have saved me a ton of tears and heartache. Lesson learned. I never realized until I had gone through this that I could not have learned what I needed to become successful. I had finally realized that failure was no longer a loss, but a huge gain. After some soul searching, I discovered that some of the biggest visionaries and history makers in the universe had failed countless times (sometimes hundreds of times). The coolest thing I realized was that almost every one of these people viewed their failures as simply opportunities for adjustment, learning lessons in what not to do, as opposed to seeing it as defeat. I wanted to share with you a list of some of the most famous people who have failed, but never gave up, in their attempt to reach their dreams. As you can see, failure always contributes to success in a positive way. It's about persevering and learning beyond your failure that creates the stepping-stone for greatness.

Abraham Lincoln - Born into poverty, Lincoln was faced with defeat throughout his life. He lost eight elections, had two failed businesses and suffered a nervous breakdown. He could have quit many times but he didn't, and he became one of the greatest presidents in the history of our country.

Orville and Wilbur Wright - Both brothers battled depression and family illness before starting a bicycle shop that would lead them to experimenting with flight. After numerous attempts at creating flying machines, and tons of failed prototypes, the brothers finally created a plane that could get airborne and stay there.

Colonel Sanders - Harland David Sanders, known as Colonel Sanders of Kentucky Fried Chicken, was unsuccessful at selling his chicken for many years. His famous secret chicken recipe was rejected 1009 times before a restaurant accepted it.

R.H. Macy - While today Macy's is one of the most iconic shopping experiences in New York City, R.H. Macy had started and failed 7 different businesses before finally reaching success with his flagship store and chain throughout the USA.

Walt Disney - Disney started his business in his home garage and his very first cartoon production went bankrupt. He was fired by the editor of a newspaper for lacking in ideas and was told he was not creative enough. He was turned down 302 times before he got financing for creating Disneyland.

J.K. Rowling- Rowling wrote *Harry Potter and the Philosopher's Stone* (the first book in the series) and was a struggling single mother on welfare and faced 12 rejections from publishers, eventually selling her book for the equivalent of $4,000. The series went on to break numerous sales records, turned into an incredibly successful film series and J.K. Rowling is now worth an estimated $1 billion.

Thomas Edison - As a boy he was told by his teacher that he was too stupid to learn anything. He failed 9,999 times before he created electricity at 10,000 tries!

Arianna Huffington - One of the most powerful businesswomen, she is no stranger to failure. While the first book she wrote was well received, her second book was rejected by 36 publishers. She is now the author of 13 books as well as the president and editor-in-chief of the *Huffington Post* Media Group.

Henry Ford - Known for his enormous success and innovation in American made cars, his earlier businesses failed and left him broke 5 times before he founded the successful Ford Motor Company.

Chapter 19
The Price Of A Dream

You have to decide what your highest priorities are and have the courage—pleasantly, smilingly, non-apologetically—to say 'no' to other things. And the way to do that is by having a bigger 'yes' burning inside.

~ Stephen Covey

I've been asked many times throughout my career, "What can I do to see my dream come true?" yet I have never been asked the question, "What can I sacrifice or give up in order to see my dream happen?" If you truly want to see your dreams come true, there will be things that you will have to give up. Whether it's time, sleep, a social life, finances, or fun, something will need to be sacrificed. If you want to live your dream it's all about sacrificing momentary pleasures for long-term gains. When I decided to go for my dream of launching my own magazine, I had to pay a considerably high price in a couple of areas to achieve what I believed was worth it.

For me, time was the biggest sacrifice I had to make in order to make a way for my dream. I had to become extremely disciplined in managing my time, literally not going out socially for months. I had to give up sleep, food, entertainment, and even seeing friends and family as much as I would have liked to. There were days where I would eat, sleep and breathe my computer, working tirelessly on creating my dream magazine, sometimes working 18-hour days! It seemed crazy to everyone else around me because at the time they didn't understand my dream.

Despite the unbelief of others, I had to persevere in working diligently because I could see the end result. Over time, all of the hard work and sacrifice paid off. Soon the magazine was sold in 37 countries and winning awards for *Best New Magazine of the Year*, by both *Aveda and SustainPrint*. We were selling out in *Whole Foods, Barnes & Noble and Target*. When the recognition started pouring in, it was amazing how those people whom at one time couldn't grasp my reasons for sacrificing everything I did suddenly appreciated the fruits of my labor. Nobody ever becomes successful by doing nothing; something's always gotta give. There will always be a high price to pay for living your dreams, but ultimately you have to decide what that will be. As much as you may want to believe that you can "have it all", trust me when I tell you this, *you cannot*. I've tried it. I believed it. The bottom line is that it's an illusion. Something will always suffer. My suggestion is to be wise about it from the beginning, and choose what you want to sacrifice, instead of letting it later choose you.

Risks vs. Rewards

"You are so lucky that you get to do your job! I wish I could do what you do!" When I'm out doing appearances, I have had people say these things to me very often, assuming I had created my career like a magician, without really understanding what it took to get there. No, I am not lucky. It took me years of hard work and 'paying my dues' in order to earn my position in fashion. I didn't just simply say, "I want to work in fashion," and it happened. I had to give up a lot to get what I wanted. I was willing to take the risk and go after my dreams, paying a very high price of sacrifice. Seeing my dream come true happened because I gave up things like going out and having fun with my friends in exchange for working, or sacrificing my vacation money in order to save money to fund my dream. I was willing to jump off the cliff without out a parachute, so to speak. I was willing to take the risk to gain the reward. I did it in faith. I had done all of the hard work to get there, as well as followed my inner compass and paid a lot of attention to what I believed my Creator was directing me to do. I gained the reward of living my dream because I was willing to step outside of my comfort zone, do the hard work and take the risk.

Be willing to dream alone.
Often when you are trying to launch your dream you are doing it alone. It can be a lonely path at times when you are leading the pack, not running along with it, mainly because it's your own dream, and so you are the one leading the process of making it happen. This quote by an unknown author explains the experience well: "A true leader has the confidence to stand alone, the courage to make tough decisions, and the compassion to listen to the needs of others. He doesn't set out to be a leader, but becomes one by the quality of his actions and the integrity of his intent. In the end, leaders are much like eagles… they do not flock; you find them one at a time."

I had a very successful CEO share with me his wisdom of leadership. "Being a leader is a lonely place. I'm alone…all the time." I knew what he meant. As a dreamer and a leader you are responsible for paving a new path. That path is not cleared yet, so it's up to you to clear it. Then others follow. But don't worry; because once you succeed suddenly everyone will want to come along for the ride. By that point you will finally become happy leading and dreaming alone.

You are not entitled.
Some people feel as if they are owed success, or feel if they can just 'meet the right person' that can help them become rich or famous, but this isn't the way to become successful. Have you ever heard someone say, "They got rich quick!" Newsflash, rich and quick do not go together. The biggest misconception about people who 'make it' is that they got there quickly and didn't do much to become successful. What's always missing from their story is what happened behind the scenes; all of the time, sacrifice and energy it took to make it happen during those invisible years when no one was watching. There was

no glory in all of the sweat equity, but for some reason some people continue to think they can make it successfully without the sacrifice. It amazes me how many people want to live their dreams but aren't willing to do what it takes to get there. They don't want to put in the effort, the pain, or the time it takes to develop them; all they want is the reward. Don't be one of those people who doesn't want to do the dirty work in order to see their dreams come true. Be willing to work for what you want to achieve.

Some people hope to hit it big by latching on to someone else's success, rather than working hard to build their own. Others want someone else to do all the work for them, without having to make the investment themselves. These types of people will always ask you all kinds of questions and want you to give them shortcuts on how to do everything, instead of figuring it out on their own. If you are one of those people who want the quick fix, then your dreams will never happen. You must want your dream so bad that you will choose it over sleep, over socializing, over having fun, and sometimes even over family events in special cases. Not that I am *at all* advising you to sacrifice your family or relationships for your dream, absolutely not. Rather, what I am saying is that sacrificing in some areas will be required for the short term, to acquire the long-term goal of living your dream. In the end you will choose what you ultimately want to give up. Your dream will never happen without sacrifice. Period.

Chapter 20
Dream Thieves:
What's Stopping You?

Our deepest fear is not that we are inadequate. Our deepest fear is that we are powerful beyond measure. It is our light, not our darkness that most frightens us. We ask ourselves, 'Who am I to be brilliant, gorgeous, talented, fabulous?' Actually, who are you not to be? You are a child of God. Your playing small does not serve the world. There's nothing enlightened about shrinking so that other people won't feel insecure around you. We are all meant to shine, as children do. We were born to make manifest the glory of God that is within us. It's not just in some of us; it's in everyone. And as we let our own light shine, we unconsciously give other people permission to do the same. As we're liberated from our own fear, our presence automatically liberates others.
— *Marianne Williamson*

While you will spend most of your energy working towards your dream coming true, at the same time there will be what I like to call 'dream thieves' working against you to try to steal, kill or destroy your dreams. Don't let this scare you. The very fact that these enemies are being disclosed is bringing you closer to your dreams, and keeping you further away from their negativity. Your only responsibility is to recognize and defeat the dream thief that's battling you. The only way for a dream thief to succeed is if you give it permission to. In the words of the late Maya Angelou, "When you know better, you do better." Now you know. Let nothing and no one ever again, stand in the way of your dreams.

Dream Thief #1 FEAR
FALSE. EVIDENCE. APPEARING. REAL. Yes, that's what fear is. It's something we feel, but has no true existence, yet fear is the #1 reason people don't pursue their dreams. Fear of rejection, fear of success, fear of failure, fear of what people think, fear of leaving a secure job, etc. There are countless fears. Fear is also the opposite of faith. You cannot have both fear and faith at the same time. If you come into agreement with fear, it will connect you to everything you are afraid of and you will never see your dreams come to pass. It's the same for your faith. If you come into agreement with faith, it will connect you to a positive life of your dreams. You can never, *ever* let fear stop you from having the faith to pursue your dream. Here are some common fears faced when dreaming:

Fear that your past reflects your future.
One of the hardest habits you may have to break is judging your future, both the people in it and it's circumstances, based on your past experiences. All of us have a history, but whether that experience is good or bad, should never dictate in your mind or heart what your future will be like. Many times the repetitive patterns we've experienced in the past are determined to shape the way we think about our future. The downfall to that is that they will create the same results. However, when you truly, in your heart, let those experiences stay in the past, not bringing them along with you as mindsets into your future, then and only then will you begin to be in the place you've

always dreamed of. Dreams are the future. They speak of hope, newness, and life. If anybody tries to remind you of your past they are certainly not worthy of you sharing your dreams with them. The past is gone, over, finished. Every day you awake is a new beginning. You are given a new opportunity for a fresh start. When dreaming, you've got to be conscious of not letting anyone talk you out of your dreams based on your past. Instead, surround yourself with people who champion you to make history and who are genuinely fighting for you, not against you. It is those who speak to your true identity. It is those who are worthy of you sharing your dreams with them. It is those special people who become your dream team. The past is gone. All things are made new.

Fear of breaking out of your comfort zone.
Did you know that one of the main reasons we don't pursue our dreams is the fear of breaking out of our comfort zone? It takes courage to quit a job, follow your passion, make a career move, walk in a direction you've never walked before, do something you've never done before! It takes a brave soul to step out of what feels comfortable and safe, choosing the unknown to follow your dream. I want to tell you today that you are equipped with the courage to break out of your comfort zone. Courage is a choice and you must choose it over fear. Now, being courageous doesn't mean you won't feel fear, it simply means choosing to walk out of your comfort zone despite the fear you are feeling! So many of us miss out on seeing our dreams come to pass because we choose that feeling of safety over experiencing that brief moment of fleeting fear that we encounter by stepping out. Today, I want you to see that courage is what will set you free and what will give your dreams wings to fly! I promise you, your dream is worth pressing past the fear of breaking out of your comfort zone.

Fear of what people think.
Whether it's your family, friends or both, everyone loves to throw their opinions at you and tell you what they think you should be

doing. Fear of people and their opinions stops many of us from moving forward into our dreams. Even if these people are the most beloved in our lives, we need to overcome the fear of not pleasing them with a desire to please God. At one time or another, we've all had fears of what people think about us. Just remember, it's not their journey, it's yours. You are the only one responsible for living your life and going after the dreams in your heart. Don't ever let the fear of what other people think steal your dreams away.

Dream Thief #2 LACK

Sometimes we don't dare to dream because of our lack of natural resources. We look at our current circumstances and think, *I can never go after my dream because I'll never enough money.* This is a lie. The truth is it will never be the 'right time' and you will never have 'enough money' when you start. There will always be obstacles in your way to make it look like it's impossible. Going after your dream will always require taking some financial risk. However, the key is to come up with a financial plan that will allow you to make your dream happen without putting your current responsibilities in jeopardy. Sometimes you may have to cut your budget in one area and re-direct some of your finances toward your dream; other times you may have to work a second job to gather up some starting capital. Whatever the case is, it can be done. Lack is never a valid excuse, because you will never have enough. If you will combat your dream thief of lack with a financial plan, you will be set up for success.

Dream Thief #3 UNBELIEF

The only place where your dream becomes impossible is in your own thinking. If you don't believe in yourself and your own dream, neither will anyone else. You must believe in the possibility of it happening before you can pursue it whole-heartedly and work towards what you desire. It is said that it is better to try and fail than never to try at all. If you don't believe it can happen, then why are you dreaming it? You must take the first step of faith if you want to see your dream come to pass. Don't ever let your dreams die because of self-proposed limitations. Do not let another day go by where you listen to the lies that you do not have what it takes, and instead turn those thoughts into truths. If you truly know in your heart that your dream is real, then don't let another day of unbelief go by. nothing is impossible to him who believes.

Dream Thief #4 DISTRACTIONS
The devil is in the distractions. Because distractions are more subtle than any other dream thief, they can be the most deadly. Day-to-day interferences can derail you from your dream without you even realizing it. If you really want to see your dream happen, you must be completely intentional and make every effort to maintain a consistent and clear focus on your dream. Distraction is one of the simplest ways to keep you from achieving your dream because it happens so easily. A phone call, scrolling through social media, emails, it's a guarantee that distraction can happen in something as simple as picking up your phone! I'm very serious in saying there will be times you must 'unplug' and turn off all electronic devices the next time you are working on your dream. That being said, you may live such a busy life that you will have to schedule a special time each day or each week for your dream. Dreams don't just happen, they happen by doing things on purpose. I cannot stress strongly enough that you must be relentlessly disciplined and steer clear of distraction, because it will steal your dream every time.

Get the losers out of your life.
You never want to have anyone in your life that is draining your dream. If someone is around you and they are constantly tearing you down, or distracting you from your dream, then they should not be offered any time in your life. If you are truly committed to your dream you should be willing to cut out anyone in your life who doesn't lift you up, isn't honest with you, or who isn't encouraging and honoring. It is your life and you have the right to exclude anyone you don't want from being

a part of it. People are typically our biggest source of distraction, so if you find that anyone continues to deplete your energy source, distract or deter you from your dream, dump them, fast—and don't feel guilty. You must protect your dream at all costs.

Dream Thief #5 WORDS

Words can be fruit or they can be poison. Choose wisely. – Proverbs

Words have creative power. Words can give life or words can kill. They can heal or destroy. Words become thoughts, and play an integral role in what manifests in your life. Look at words like seeds planted in the garden of your mind and heart. The creative power of words can both grow and flourish your dreams into a blossoming fruit-bearing tree, or they can cripple and whither away your dreams into a diseased tree, shriveled up at the roots. I've watched too many dreams nearly get aborted because of other people's unbelieving words, or because of their own destructive self-talk.

When it comes to dreams, we need to take the power of words seriously. We can never let our own words, or the words of another, allow us to believe a lie that will convince us to abort our dream. Decide that you won't let your dreams die because of what somebody else told you. People will always try to talk you out of your dream. Here is a common list of lies you may hear when you share your dream with someone else or even hear in your own head.

"You're crazy!"

"That's impossible."

"You've lost your mind."

"You're not smart enough."

"You're too old."

"You're too young."

"You can't afford it."

"You need to be realistic."

"You don't have what it takes."

"Do you think you're special?"

"You don't have enough time."

"You're an average person, nothing happens to average people."

"There's too much competition."

"That idea will never sell."

"That's been done before."

"It's never gonna happen."

"It's too hard."

"Grow up."

"You have a family to provide for. You can't possibly take care of your kids *and* do this."

"No one in your family ever did anything important, why should it happen to you?"

"Stop Dreaming. Face reality."

"Get your head out of the clouds."

"You are living in a fantasy world."

"You can't possibly quit your job."

"You don't come from a family of risk-takers. Be practical."

"One day."

And the list goes on…

DON'T EVER ALLOW ANYONE ELSE THE POWER TO FRAME YOUR FUTURE AND DETERMINE YOUR DREAMS. YOUR DREAMS BELONG TO YOU, THE DREAMER. DON'T GIVE THEM AWAY.

Dream Thief #6 JEALOUSY

You have to protect your dream. Your dream is a like a baby. Just like you wouldn't hand off your baby to a total stranger, it's the same for your dream. Dreams must be guarded and protected until they are ready to be birthed. Contrary to what you may believe, not everyone will be as happy about your dream as you are. In fact, you may encounter just the opposite from people, some of whom may even be your family or friends. When you first start going after your dream you will be filled with so much excitement that your first instinct will be to want to share your dream with someone else, but be warned. People, while not all of them intending to be this way, can become jealous, angry, resentful, and envious that you are willing to take the step that they are afraid to. Watch their reaction. They will either sit there in silent resentment unable to speak a word, or become loud and obnoxious, dumbing down your idea and trying to convince you it is stupid and a waste of time. *DO NOT*, I repeat, *do not,* take these people seriously and do not for one-minute let their words or attitude take root in your heart.

In the past I've definitely been burned by sharing some of my dreams with people I thought I could trust. I had to learn the very difficult lesson about who your real friends are. You see while to my face these 'friends' may have seemed happy for me to my face, inside they were seething with jealousy just wishing I would fail. In a few instances, I would later find out that they either stole my idea for themselves, or that they were speaking negative words behind my back. Both of these scenarios were very difficult experiences to go through because I had trusted the people I shared them with. I've only included this reality in this book because I want you to avoid going through the same painful process.

I hope you heed my advice about not sharing your dream with anyone in its early stages of development unless you truly know in your spirit that they want what's best for you. Even if you are the type of person who is happy watching others succeed, you must understand, as sad as it may be, that not all people share that same perspective as you. *You will never take away from someone else's light when you shine your own*. People who feel like they are losing because you are winning are filled with insecurity and lack of love. You can't get caught up in their negativity, even when it comes against you. We should be happy to see one another succeed, especially those we know personally. There is enough room for everyone to win.

Dream Thief #7 GIANTS

Giants come in many forms, from competition to opposition. They arrive in the form of people; your parents, a spouse, a pastor, a friend, a co-worker, etc. Think of a giant as a bully. They never really plan on doing anything, but they come along to intimidate you into thinking they can steal your stuff and destroy you. Giants will always try to talk you out of your dream. Many times, these people who are giants love you the most, and may not even realize that they are being a giant in your life because they think they are "Doing it for your own good," or "Don't want to see you let down," or "want you to be practical." Here's an example of how someone can be a giant and try to talk you out of your own dream.

Carrie has a dream of building an afterschool community program for children, to give them a place to go while their parents are still at work. She is extremely passionate about creating something special like this because when she was a child, both of her parents worked and therefore each day after school she was forced to sit in an empty house until they arrived home. One of the biggest pains that plagued Carrie was that while she had to stay inside, she could see the other neighborhood children playing together outside. Unfortunately, this experience caused her to become quite introverted in school because she knew she was never allowed to play or interact after school. Slowly, she guarded her heart and became a loner. Fast forward to today, now that Carrie is an adult, she still feels a lot of pain from these memories and deep within her spirit she yearns to 'do something' for children that would help them avoid ever feeling how she felt. Deep down, Carrie knows that she can truly make a difference by creating a program like this.

With that excitement she decides to share her idea with her friends and family. Unfortunately, because they have never walked in her shoes, they cannot relate to her idea or her passion and completely minimize the need to create something like this.

Carrie walks away feeling defeated, despite knowing deep down that she can help so many children in need. And while she believes with all of her heart something like this needs to exist, she puts more value on what her friends and family are saying over what she believes in her heart, and therefore she buries her dream.

Do you see how easy it is to share your dream with someone else only to have them wreck it? Any one of us could easily listen to what the people in our lives are saying and because we value our relationship with them end up believing that they know what's best for us, therefore forfeiting our own dreams. Unfortunately many times, it is those closest to us that don't believe in our vision. It could be our parents, a spouse, a partner, a best friend, anyone. Most times those who love you may not even realize that they are not being supportive; they just may not possess the same fire in your belly that propels you, or they have more of a 'play it safe' mentality and don't even recognize that they are not on your side. They will tell you that they are "Doing it for your own good," or "Don't want to see you get hurt," or "Want you to be practical." They may claim they "Want to protect you," "Don't want to see you disappointed," "Think you should be realistic," or "Maintain a safe job or position," putting stability ahead of a dream. The key is that, no matter what anyone tells you, ultimately, you've got to get to the place where it only matters that you can see your dream, regardless of whether or not others can appreciate it. It's up to you to truly become so secure in trusting what your inner compass is telling you that, no matter what anyone says, even if they love you, you have the confidence to listen to your own voice, and God's voice above all.

Chapter 21
The Attitude of A Winner

No matter how you feel. Get up. Dress up. Show up.
And never give up.
~Regina Brett

It is said that your attitude determines your altitude. When it comes to your dreams you must have a can-do, right believing, positive attitude and be ready to press on to the finish line! With every dream there comes a time when you will start to wonder if your dream is ever going to happen. There will be signs everywhere that make it look like your dreams are impossible. However, I know that what's even bigger than the impossible is POSSIBLE with a God-given dream. It's easy to give up on your dreams when it's been too long, but do not ever let go of the dream that's inside of you, even when thoughts come your way telling you that it's never going to happen. Life's pressures will come with so much temptation to quit, but you cannot. No matter how many times you have been disappointed in the past you must maintain the attitude of a winner. Quitting is never an option. I want to assure you that, even if it has taken 5, 10 or even 20 years, your dream isn't dead and it's not over. God will always finish what He started in you. God has not brought you this far to leave you. Just because you don't see a way doesn't mean God doesn't have a way. The most powerful force in the universe is at work in your life and wants to bring your dreams to pass. The only time your dream is dead is when you are! What you think is dead is only buried, and is about to bloom into something beautiful. Only a winning attitude can keep you going even when you can't see the finish line in sight! You are a winner, and winners never quit and quitters never win!

I'll never forget the day I was once again questioning whether my dreams were really going to happen or not. That day in particular, some things were weighing very heavy on my heart. I wondered, *Is it all over?* Were my dreams dead and gone? Then suddenly, out of nowhere, I received a text message linked to a YouTube video entitled *DREAM* by producer Mateusz M. It was a montage from various movies that showed the journey of a dream with a voice-over about what a person goes through who is pursuing their dream. What I can tell you is that from the moment I began watching this video my heart exploded with emotion, mainly because it was the most incredible re-minder of what the journey of a dream is truly like. I knew it all too well from living out past dreams. Watching this video in that moment brought me such peace. The words in this message were so powerful that I felt I must share them with you.

After reading this, I hope you get to watch the video on YouTube for yourself. Here is the link: https://www.youtube.com/watch?v=g-jwWYX7Jlo

DREAM
Transcript from a film adapted by Mateusz M.

I don't know what that dream is that you have. I don't care how disappointing it might have been as you've been working toward that dream, but that dream that you're holding in your mind, that it's possible! That some of you already know that it's hard, it's not easy. It's hard changing your life.

That in the process of working on your dreams you are going to incur a lot of disappointment, a lot of failure, a lot of pain. There are moments you will doubt yourself, and say God why? Why is that happening to me? I'm just trying to take care of my children, my family, I'm not trying to steal or rob from anybody. Why did this have to happen to me?

For those of you that have experienced hardships, don't give up on your dream.

The rough times are gonna come, but they have not come to stay, they have come to pass!

Greatness is not this wonderful, esoteric, elusive God-like feature that only the special among us will ever taste. It's something that truly exists in all of us.

It's very important for you to believe that YOU are the one.

Most people they raise a family, they earn a living and then they die.

They stop growing, they stop working on themselves, they stop stretching. They stop pushing themselves.

Then a lot of people like to complain, but they don't want to do anything about their situation.

Most people don't work on their dreams. Why? One is because of fear. Fear of failure; what if they don't work out? And the fear of success; what if they do and I can't handle it? These are not risk-takers.

You spend so much time with other people. You spend so much time trying to get people to like you. You know other people more than you know yourself. You studied them, you know about them, you want to hang out like them, you want to be just like them. And you know what? You've invested so much time on them you don't know who you are. I challenge you to spend time by yourself.

It's necessary that you get the losers out of your life, if you want to live your dream!

But people running towards their dream, life has a special kind of meaning.

When you become the right person, what you do is start to separate yourself from people. You begin to have a certain uniqueness. As long as you follow other people, as long as you being a copycat, you will never, ever be the best copycat in the world, but you will be the best you can be. I challenge you to define your value.

(Regarding your dream)That everyone won't see it. That everybody won't join you. That everybody won't have the vision. It's necessary to know that, that you are an uncommon breed. It's necessary that you align yourself with people and attract people into your business who are hungry, people who are unstoppable and unreasonable, people who refuse to live life just as it is, who want more! The people that are living their dreams are finding winners to attach themselves to.

They are the people that know if it's going to happen it's up to them.

If you want to be more successful, if you want to have and do the stuff you have never done before, then I'm asking you to invest in YOU.

Someone's opinion of you does not have to become your reality.

You don't have to go through life being a victim.

Even though you face disappointments, you have to know within yourself that I can do this, even if no one sees it for you, I must see it for myself.

This is what I believe and I'm willing to die for it. Period.

No matter how bad it is or how bad it gets, I'm going to make it! I want to represent an idea. I want to represent possibilities.

Some of you right now, you want to go to the next level "I want to counsel. I want to be an engineer. I want to be a doctor". Listen to me: You can't get to that level economically until you start to invest in your mind. You're not reading books. I'm challenging you all to go to conferences. I dare you to invest time; I dare you to be alone. I dare you to spend time an hour getting to know yourself.

When you become who you are, the person you were created to be, designed to be who you were designed to be. When you become an individual, what you do is you take yourself and start separating yourself from other people.

I challenge you to get to a place where people do not like you or don't even want to bother with you anymore. Why? Cause you are not concerned with making other people happy, because you're trying to blow up. You are trying to get to the next level. I need you to invest in your mind.

If you are still talking about your dream. If you are still talking about your goals but you have not done anything,

JUST TAKE THE FIRST STEP.

You can make your parents proud, you can make your school proud, you can touch millions of people's lives, *and the world will never be the same again because you came this way!*

Don't let anybody steal your dream!

After we face a rejection, and a "NO", or we have a meeting and no one shows up, or somebody says, "You can count on me" and they don't come through? What if we have that kind of attitude when our car is repossessed, nobody believes in you, you've lost again and again and again and the lights are cut off but you are still looking at your dream, reviewing it every day and saying to yourself; *"IT'S NOT OVER UNTIL I WIN!"*

YOU CAN LIVE YOUR DREAM!

Chapter 22
The Heart of a Champion

Champions are not the ones who always win races - champions are the ones who get out there and try. And try harder the next time. 'Champion' is a state of mind. They are devoted. They compete to best themselves as much if not more than they compete to best others.
~ Simon Sinek

To achieve your dream you've got to have the heart of a champion. A conqueror's mentality. A warrior's spirit. A champion looks for opportunities to make things better, not reasons why they will stay stuck. They don't complain about what they don't have, but instead they make the most of what they do have. They don't make excuses for not making their dream happen, or let fear, lack of time or money, unbelief, wasting time on social media, or anything get in the way of finishing what they started! You see, it is always exciting to start a dream, but it's a priceless experience to finish one. I have seen so many people begin their dreams because they are so pumped up emotionally with passion, yet they lack the endurance and faith that's required to complete it.

A champion knows there will be times when you will have to fight to see your dream come true. You must possess a fighter's stamina and know that no matter how many times you get knocked down, you will *always* get back up. John Osteen, said it like this: *"Fight for your dreams. Fight, Fight, Fight through, so you can say in the end,* *the dream is true. "*As a dreamer, having the heart of a champion will give you the endurance of an athlete who doesn't want to quit. Like a runner in a race, the last part of your dream will feel like the toughest to push through. You are exhausted, thirsty, and worn-out, and the finish line seems so far away—yet it's so close! It's in this time that fight or flight kicks in and your body and mind will want to cave in and quit...*but you cannot give up on your dream now*! Just because you face challenges, feel defeated or have become beaten down does not mean you should take it as a 'sign' to stop. It just means you need to take a break, a pause, or a rest. Remember, you are a champion! Take some time to clear your mind to help you regain the strength and stamina so you can persevere till the end. I love how author Sarah Kay puts it: *"Life will hit you hard in the face, wait for you to get back up just so it can kick you in the stomach. But getting the wind knocked out of you is the only way to remind your lungs how much they like the taste of air."* Yes, that sums it up. You will learn to love the taste of air, instead of looking to resist the punch! Let the process of going after your dreams make you grow into somebody who not only regains strength from his weaknesses, but also develops the true heart of a champion. Victory is yours!

Chapter 23
The Spirit Of A Finisher

Dreams aren't finish lines to be reached at the close of a race. They don't suddenly materialize, fulfilled, where the road ends. The entire journey is included in the dream — all of it from beginning to forevermore.
~ Richelle E. Goodrich

I am not sure that we ever 'arrive'. What I do know for sure is that we arrive at different destinations at varied points in our life, and some of them are when a dream comes true. When you live through the entire process of designing your dream and you actually experience it become your reality, it's one of the most amazing feelings in the world! There is an unspeakable joy when a dream you have waited for your entire life becomes complete. Your heart beats faster than it ever has. You smile wider than you ever thought you could. You feel as if you can conquer the world and there is exuberance inside of you that's never been there before, making you feel like you would relive it all over again if you could! The fact is YOU MADE IT! You hit the finish line. Every battle conquered; every challenge won. Total victory! You made it to your own personal Super Bowl and YOU won the game!

Right now I feel such an out-of-body excitement for you as I watch you step into new things, new seasons and new places. No matter what size your dream, big or small, the utter gratification and ecstasy of having it come true will leave you with a feeling of elation you'll never want to forget. So, today, soak in that moment! Embrace that winning feeling. Relish this precious season of your success! Take the time to thank your Creator for seeing you through to the end, and be grateful to those who've helped you along the way. Today is your day to enjoy the pure joy of a dream come true! I know one day yours will, if it hasn't already!

DESIGN YOUR DREAM.

There is no passion to be found playing small, in settling for a life that is less than the one you are capable of living.

~ *Nelson Mandela*

My Designer

When I speak of God, you must know that God is my Designer, my Creator, my Master Artist and the biggest Dreamer I know. He rocks because He is not at all about religion, but about relationship. He is not about a Sunday hour mass. He is about an every day, every second, super fun, thrilling, loving, exciting roller coaster ride of awesomeness! He is an amazing Father who leads me throughout every step of this life's journey so I can follow His son Jesus into my eternity. He's my counselor, my encourager, my closest friend, my leader, my provider and my protector. He created you and me like the stars in the sky, knowing each one of us by name before we were birthed in our mother's womb. He is God, and I can't say He physically sits next to me every day and has coffee with me, but I can say that every morning I sit with Him and have coffee and sometimes tea, and He is always there listening and guiding my heart; leading me to do what's right and good in this world. He unconditionally loves you and me more than anything else He has ever created. He wants nothing more than to give you the desires of your heart and help you live out the dreams He gave you, only so you can know how great His love is for you! I'm in love with *Love*, because that's what and who God is, UNCONDITIONAL *LOVE*. And He's good, *all* of the time. I pray you get to know Him like I do. If you do, I promise you that your life will be forever changed for the better.

111

Acknowledgements

I want to thank everyone who has helped me along this dream journey. Thank you for taking the time to help me live out another one of my dreams, only so I can help you live yours!

First of all, this book wouldn't even exist without my Creator. This book was a divine download and I gave it my fingerprints and a voice. I'm graced with the honor and privilege of being able to write and share it with you, praying it will help you live out your dreams and help you discover your divine purpose for living. I believe it is my calling to serve you. Thank you.

To my children Sebastian Bo, Hope Rain and Isabella Star; you are my biggest dream, my loves and my life. Your precious hearts inspire me everyday to leave you a legacy that goes beyond my human comprehension. You three are my stars. Living everyday life with you is a reminder to me of how good God's grace really is. I am so blessed to have you and be able to dream with you!

To my parents; Patrick and Joann. My biggest fans, my supporters, and my rocks. You guys are a heavenly tag team that birthed me into this earthly existence and now you are forever along with me for the ride! Words can never be enough to thank you for all you have done. You funded my very first dream of going to college in NYC to attend F.I.T, and then my second dream to Paris, London and Milan to study my passion of fashion! You never stopped believing in me. Thank you! I love you.

To my brothers; Patrick and Joseph. Thank you for always busting my chops to the point where you fueled me to do something great and get out of the house. You are both incredibly talented and I love seeing you soar. Love you both, always.

To my Godmother 'Auntie' Gloria; my best friend, my confidant, my prayer warrior, my fashion partner, and my reason for why I needed to finish this book already (wink wink CC)! Thank you for your limitless love, faithful prayers and endless encouragement you have sowed into me since I was a child. You truly are my 'God' mama. xo

To my Grandma Glo; Your love and light shine so bright. I pray one day I can be as positive and joyful as you are! Thank you for your encouragement and belief in me, along with your relentless reminders that my gifts and talents are in my 'career' and not in the laundry room (wink wink). xo

To my Grandpa Bo; I miss you tons! I still have that Vogue article you gave me on my desk, I cherish it. I inherited your passion for the ocean, your endless desire to travel and see the world like you and Grandma did, and your love of people. I love all of it! Thank you. xo Gina-babe.

To my Grandma Dickie; I can never say enough thanks for your endless hours of prayers and love you put in for me. Your laugh will forever be echoed in my heart. I had the awesome experience of living with you and Grandpa after college and it was a time in my life I will forever cherish. xo

To my Grandpa Joe; I miss you tons! I've included your words in this book and I will eternally remember why I have two ears and one mouth. Your priceless wisdom forever changed my life. Thank you for all your love and strength. xo Your #1.

Special thanks to my designer, Jeremiah Lanska. Your talents and integrity are unmatched! I can't ever thank you enough for all of your hard work and dedication you've put in working with me. Thank you!

Thank you to my photographer, Anthony Bagileo, who has known me my entire life yet had to wait 5 years to take this picture! Ha. Thanks for your patience and talent. So happy you embraced your passion for shooting!

To all of my dear friends and loved ones who've helped me along this dream journey I am so grateful for your friendship, love and support. Thank you for always being there. Real friends are priceless.

It is quite hard to list every person who has ever influenced me in becoming who I am today, because I believe everyone who has crossed my path has contributed in some way to my growth and success in this life. For all of you unmentioned, I am aware of you in my heart. Thank you.

What lies before us and what lies behind us are small matters compared to what lies within us. And when you bring what is within out into the world, miracles happen.

~ Henry David Thoreau

About the Author,
Gina La Morte

Gina La Morte is a Celebrity Fashion Stylist, Speaker and Author who has a heart to set people free and unlock their God-given dreams, releasing them into their divine destiny. Gina has worked as a Celebrity Fashion Stylist for *O, The Oprah magazine, People StyleWatch, W magazine, Nordstrom, Neiman Marcus, Saks Fifth Avenue, Bloomingdales and more.* She has attended both the *Academy Awards* and the *Emmy's*. Her work has been seen by millions on *The View, Bravo, MTV, CBS, ABC and FOX morning shows. Gina's expertise has been featured in countless media outlets some of which include USA Today, The LA Times, MORE magazine, KTLA, Life & Style, Associated Press, One on One with Steve Adubato, Fitness magazine, OK! magazine, and Yahoo.*

In 2008, she founded *Boho* magazine. *Boho* was an environmentally conscious fashion publication printed on 100% post-consumer waste paper, featuring fashion designers, dreamers, handmade artisans, and social entrepreneurs who are committed to making a difference by giving back or going green. *Boho* was a two-time award-winning publication, receiving both the *AVEDA* award and the *Sustainprint* award for '*New Magazine of the Year*'. *Boho* was distributed throughout the USA and in 37 other countries. It was sold in retailers including *Barnes & Noble, Whole Foods, Target, Duane Reade, CVS* and food markets & drugstores nationwide.

Gina is passionate about giving back to both her local community and internationally. Some charities she has assisted in the past have been The *Nelson Mandela Foundation, Dress for Success, JBWS, and Nomi Network*. She is committed to partnering with those who can release freedom to women and children currently being trafficked around the world.

For more on Gina please visit her website

www.GinaLaMorte.com

For Speaking engagements contact:

info@ginalamorte.com

www.GinaLaMorte.com

Twitter   @Gina_LaMorte
Instagram @GinaLaMorte
Facebook @Gina La Morte
Pinterest @Bohomag
@GinaLaMorte

Words

"I have had the pleasure of knowing Gina for over 5 years, and feel completely blessed by her ability to translate your vision and dreams into her own words and creative power. Gina is a treasure to my heart and I trust her with my dreams and desires because she believes in the power of what God can do with each one of us. Gina never gives up on my dreams and she is my pleasant reminder that God has gifted me with people that are here to reinforce the truth about who I am. Gina is one of those sweet reminders that God's vision in my heart, in dream form, will have its place here on earth. "

~ Sybil Clark-Amuti, Chief Strategy Officer
Impact Republic
New York, New York

"Gina La Morte has fashioned a winning book for you! Designing Your Dream will open the windows of creativity and empower you to see the possibilities in discovering your destiny. Packed with deep insight and years of personal experience, Gina skillfully coaches you through your own breakthrough. Gina helped me discover a personal dream of mine!"

~ Doug Addison, Author
Understand Your Dreams Now
Los Angeles, California

"At the beginning of this year, something inside of me came to life and said, "I want more! I want to fulfill all my dreams and I will not stop until I do!" Then you launched Designing Your Dream academy! It's amazing what all has happened as a result of your teachings...in only 4 months! I can't wait to see what happens in the next 4! I love being a part of like-minded people like you Gina. Thank you for gathering us!"

~ Cara Linn Bowling, President
Pink Velvet Sweets
Amarillo, Texas

Walk with the dreamers,
the believers, the courageous,
the cheerful, the planners,
the doers, the successful people
with their head in the clouds
and their feet on the ground.
Let their spirit ignite a fire
within you to leave this world
better than when you found it.

~Wilfred Peterson

SHARE YOUR VISION.

FOLLOW YOUR PASSION.

LIVE YOUR DREAM.